WINTER PUDDINGS & TREATS

Edited by Louise Steele and Wendy James
Home economist Gilly Cubitt

ORBIS PUBLISHING London

Introduction

Whether you're looking for everyday ideas or something rather more special, here is a range of delicious puddings and desserts, cakes, biscuits and confectionery to suit any occasion.

Both imperial and metric measures are given for each recipe; you should follow only one set of measures as they are not direct conversions. All spoon measures are level unless otherwise stated. Pastry quantities are based on the amount of flour used.

Photographs were supplied by Editions Atlas, Editions Atlas/Masson, Editions Atlas/Zadora, Barry Bullough, Melvin Grey, Archivio IGDA, Dave Jordan, Lavinia Press Agency, Orbis GmbH, Roger Phillips

The material in this book has previously appeared in *The Complete Cook*

First published 1985 in Great Britain by Orbis Publishing Limited, 20-22 Bedfordbury, London WC2

ISBN 0-85613-750-2
Printed in Italy

Contents

Hot pies, puddings and desserts

Traditional apple pie

Overall timing 1 hour

Freezing Not suitable

To serve 4–6

8 oz	Plain flour	225 g
	Pinch of salt	
4 oz	Butter	125 g
1½ lb	Cooking apples	700 g
4 tbsp	Brown sugar	4×15 ml
½ teasp	Ground cinnamon	2.5 ml
¼ teasp	Grated nutmeg	1.25 ml
¼ teasp	Ground cloves	1.25 ml
2 oz	Sultanas	50 g
	Milk	
1 tbsp	Caster sugar	15 ml

Preheat oven to 400°F (200°C) Gas 6.

Sift flour and salt together into a bowl and rub in butter. Add enough water to mix to a firm dough.

Peel, core and slice apples into a bowl. Add brown sugar, spices and sultanas. Put mixture in buttered 2 pint (1.1 litre) pie dish. Sprinkle over 2 tbsp (2×15 ml) of water.

Roll out dough and cover pie. Decorate with dough trimmings. Brush with milk and sprinkle with caster sugar.

Bake for 20 minutes. Reduce heat to 350°F (180°C) Gas 4 and bake for a further 20 minutes.

Panisses

Overall timing 50 minutes

Freezing Suitable before deep frying

Makes 16

1 pint	Water	560 ml
6 oz	Chickpea flour	175 g
4 tbsp	Oil	4×15 ml
	Pinch of salt	
	Oil for deep frying	

Bring the water to the boil in a pan. Whisk in the chickpea flour, using a wire whisk. Add the oil and salt and stir continuously over a gentle heat till mixture thickens. Spread the mixture to a thickness of 1/4 inch (6mm) on the baking tray. Allow to cool.

Heat the oil in the deep-fryer to 340°F (170°C). Using a cutter or glass as a guide, cut out rounds from the cooled chickpea paste and lift off tray.

Deep-fry a few at a time in the hot oil for 5 minutes or until golden brown. Drain on kitchen paper and keep warm while frying the rest.

To serve, sprinkle with sugar and serve hot.

Chocolate bread pudding

Overall timing 1 hour

Freezing Suitable

To serve 8–10

9 oz	Fresh white or brown bread	250 g
½ pint	Milk	300 ml
3	Eggs	3
5 oz	Butter	150 g
4 oz	Caster sugar	125 g
½ teasp	Cinnamon	2.5 ml
	Ground cloves	
	Grated rind of ½ a lemon	
1 tbsp	White rum (optional)	15 ml
2 oz	Grated chocolate	50 g
1 oz	Cocoa	25 g

Crumble the bread into a bowl and add the milk. Leave to soak. Separate the eggs. In another bowl, cream together butter and sugar and then beat in the egg yolks. Add the breadcrumb mixture, cinnamon, pinch of ground cloves, lemon rind, rum if using, chocolate and cocoa. Mix well together.

Whisk the egg whites till stiff. Fold into the pudding mixture. Grease a 2½ pint (1.5 litre) fluted ring mould or basin with margarine, pour in the mixture, cover with foil or greaseproof paper, greased and tied on firmly. Place in saucepan with boiling water nearly up to rim, cover and steam gently for 40 minutes.

To serve, turn pudding out and serve hot with whipped cream flavoured with rum, or custard.

Bettelman

Overall timing 50 minutes

Freezing Not suitable

To serve 4–6

1½ lb	Cooking apples	700 g
¼ pint	Water	150 ml
2 oz	Nibbed almonds	50 g
2 oz	Sultanas	50 g
7 oz	Wholemeal bread	200 g
4 oz	Caster sugar	125 g
2 oz	Butter	50 g

Peel apples and slice into a saucepan. Add water, almonds and sultanas. Cover and cook over a gentle heat for 10 minutes. Remove from heat.

Preheat the oven to 425°F (220°C) Gas 7. Crumble the bread into a bowl and mix in half the sugar.

Grease an ovenproof dish with some of the butter and spread half the bread mixture over the base. Cover with apple mixture then top with remaining bread. Sprinkle on rest of sugar and dot with remaining butter. Cook for about 20 minutes in the centre of the oven. Serve hot.

Galette des rois

Overall timing 1 hour plus pastry preparation time

Freezing Suitable: before freezing

To serve 6–8

1 lb	Puff pastry	225 g
Frangipane filling		
2 oz	Caster sugar	50 g
1 oz	Soft butter	25 g
1	Egg	1
2 oz	Ground almonds	50 g
	Almond essence	
1 tbsp	Rum or lemon juice	15 ml
2 tbsp	Icing sugar	2×15 ml
1	Bean or almond	1

Cut puff pastry into two halves. Roll out each piece in a circular shape about 1 inch (2cm) thick. Use a plate as a guide to make two circles. Cover, chill for 30 minutes.

Meanwhile prepare frangipane filling by kneading together the sugar, butter, egg yolk, ground almonds, few drops almond essence and rum or lemon juice.

Preheat the oven to 450°F (230°C) Gas 8. Wet a baking tray and place one round of pastry on it. Brush the edge with egg white.

Spread the frangipane on the pastry to within 1 inch (2.5cm) of the edge. Place a bean or an almond on filling and cover with the second pastry round. Press the edges together, then crimp edges with a knife. Brush the top of galette with egg white, then mark a swirl pattern with a sharp knife.

Place galette in oven and cook for 15 minutes. Remove and dust with icing sugar, then return to top shelf of oven for 3–4 minutes to glaze the top.

Croquettes de semoule à l'orange

Overall timing 30 minutes plus cooling

Freezing Suitable before frying

To serve 6

1 pint	Milk	560 ml
	Salt	
	Grated rind of 1 orange	
4 oz	Semolina	125 g
4 oz	Caster sugar	125 g
2	Eggs	2
2 oz	Dried breadcrumbs	50 g
2 oz	Unsalted butter	50 g
2 tbsp	Oil	2×15 ml
5 tbsp	Marmalade	5×15 ml
2 tbsp	Water or orange liqeur	2×15 ml

Warm the milk in a saucepan with a pinch of salt and the orange rind. Pour in the semolina and bring to the boil, stirring. Stir over a low heat for 5–7 minutes till mixture thickens. Stir in all but 2 tbsp (2×15 ml) of the sugar.

Remove pan from the heat. Separate eggs and beat yolks into semolina. Pour into a greased bowl, cover and leave to cool.

Shape the semolina into croquettes 1 inch (2.5cm) thick and 2 inches (5cm) long. Lightly beat the egg whites and coat the croquettes, then roll them in the breadcrumbs till evenly coated. Heat the butter and oil in the frying pan, add the croquettes and fry till golden on all sides, turning occasionally. Drain on kitchen paper, then sprinkle with remaining sugar. Heat the marmalade in a small saucepan with the water or liqueur. Serve with warm croquettes.

Banana tart

Overall timing 1 hour 50 minutes

Freezing Not suitable

To serve 8		
7 oz	**Plain flour**	**200 g**
½ teasp	**Baking powder**	**2.5 ml**
½ teasp	**Salt**	**2.5 ml**
3 tbsp	**Caster sugar**	**3×15 ml**
3½ oz	**Butter**	**100 g**
1	**Medium egg**	**1**
Filling		
3 oz	**Seedless raisins** *or*	**75 g**
2 oz	**Stoned dates**	**50 g**
2 tbsp	**Rum**	**2×15 ml**
4	**Ripe bananas**	**4**
2	**Eggs**	**2**
3 oz	**Caster sugar**	**75 g**
4 fl oz	**Double cream**	**113 ml**
2 oz	**Split almonds**	**50 g**

Sift flour, baking powder, salt and sugar into a bowl. Rub in butter. Add egg with a little water if necessary to bind to a dough. Chill for 1 hour.

Put raisins, or chopped dates, to steep in rum.

Preheat the oven to 400°F (200°C) Gas 6.

Roll out dough and use to line 9 inch (23cm) fluted flan ring. Prick and bake blind for 10 minutes. Remove beans and paper, and bake for a further 5 minutes. Remove from oven.

Drain dried fruit, reserving rum. Peel bananas and cut in diagonal slices. Cover bottom of pastry case with the bananas and most of the dried fruit.

Whisk eggs and sugar together till pale and thick. Whip cream with reserved rum. Blend both mixtures together and pour over the fruit in pastry case. Scatter over almonds and reserved dried fruit.

Bake for 25 minutes until puffed, golden brown and set. Serve hot with single cream.

Grapefruit soufflés

Overall timing 45 minutes

Freezing Not suitable

To serve 6

6	**Grapefruit**	6
3 oz	**Butter**	75 g
2 oz	**Plain flour**	50 g
	Finely grated rind of 1 orange	
1–2 oz	**Caster sugar**	25–50 g
3	**Eggs**	3

Preheat oven to 375°F (190°C) Gas 5.

Slice tops off grapefruit and squeeze juice out of flesh very gently – measure out ½ pint (300 ml). Remove flesh and membranes with grapefruit knife and discard. Retain shells.

Melt the butter in a saucepan, stir in the flour and cook for 2 minutes. Gradually stir in the grapefruit juice. Bring to the boil and cook, stirring, for 2 minutes or until the sauce thickens. Add orange rind and sugar and stir until sugar dissolves. Remove from heat and leave to cool slightly.

Separate the eggs and beat the yolks into the sauce. Whisk the egg whites in a bowl till stiff, then carefully fold into the sauce mixture.

Place empty grapefruit shells in a foil-lined bun tin and fill with the mixture. Bake for 15–20 minutes till well risen and golden. Serve immediately.

Sussex pond pudding

Overall timing 4 hours

Freezing Not suitable

To serve 6–8

8 oz	**Self-raising flour**	**225 g**
4 oz	**Shredded suet**	**125 g**
¼ pint	**Milk**	**150 ml**
4 oz	**Butter**	**125 g**
4 oz	**Soft brown sugar**	**125 g**
1	**Large thin-skinned lemon**	**1**

Mix the flour and suet in large bowl. Add the milk a little at a time to give a soft, but not sticky, dough. Knead the dough lightly. Roll out three-quarters of the dough and use to line a well-greased 2½ pint (1.5 litre) pudding basin.

Cream the butter and sugar together until fluffy and spread half the mixture over the bottom and sides of the pastry.

Pierce the lemon all over with a fine skewer (to help the juices run out during cooking). Stand the lemon upright in centre of the basin, then add the remaining creamed mixture.

Roll out remaining dough and cover the filling, sealing pastry edges well. Cover the basin with a piece of greased greaseproof paper which has a large pleat to allow for expansion. Cover with pleated foil and tie with string, making a handle to aid removal from saucepan.

Place basin in saucepan containing 3 inches (7.5cm) boiling water. Cover and leave to boil for 3½ hours, topping up with extra boiling water as it evaporates.

Lift basin from saucepan. Remove foil and paper and run a knife round the sides of the basin to release the pudding. Invert on to a warmed serving plate and serve hot with pouring custard or cream.

Apricot pancakes

Overall timing 45 minutes

Freezing Suitable: fill pancakes after thawing and reheating

To serve 4

2	Eggs	2
¼ pint	Milk	150 ml
2fl oz	Water	60 ml
3 oz	Plain flour	75 g
1 oz	Caster sugar	25 g
	Vanilla essence	
	Pinch of salt	
3½ oz	Butter or lard	100 g
8 tbsp	Apricot jam	8×15 ml
	Icing sugar	
1 oz	Ground hazelnuts	25 g

Put eggs, milk and water into a bowl. Add the flour, caster sugar, a few drops of vanilla essence and salt. Whisk or beat well together until creamy and smooth.

Melt a knob of butter or lard in a small frying pan. Pour in a little of the batter and spread in a thin layer over the pan, using a spatula. When underside is cooked, flip the pancake over to brown the other side.

As soon as each pancake is ready, spread with apricot jam and roll up. Put on to a dish and keep warm in the oven while you cook the other pancakes, adding more butter or lard to the pan as necessary.

Before serving, dredge with icing sugar and sprinkle with ground hazelnuts or chopped nuts of your choice.

Flamed bananas

Overall timing 5–6 minutes

Freezing Not suitable

To serve 4

4	Bananas	4
6 tbsp	Caster sugar	6×15 ml
	Plain flour	
1	Large egg	1
1½ oz	Butter	40 g
8	Glacé cherries	8
3 tbsp	Kirsch or Cognac	3×15 ml

Peel the bananas and halve lengthways. Sprinkle with sugar, reserving a little sugar for later.

Dip bananas in flour and then into the beaten egg. Dip once again in the flour and then fry bananas in melted butter, over a medium heat, until golden on both sides.

Place bananas on a warm serving dish and decorate with the glacé cherries. Sprinkle with the reserved sugar and pour over the warmed Kirsch or Cognac. Flame, using a long lighted taper, and serve immediately.

Apple puffs

Overall timing 1 hour 10 minutes plus thawing time for pastry

Freezing Not suitable

To serve 4

7½ oz	**Packet of frozen puff pastry**	**212 g**
1 lb	**Red Delicious apples**	**450 g**
3 oz	**Butter**	**75 g**
3 oz	**Caster sugar**	**75 g**
2 tbsp	**Cold water**	**2×15 ml**
1	**Egg yolk**	**1**
1 tbsp	**Milk**	**15 ml**

Thaw out pastry according to instructions on packet. Preheat oven to 425°F (220°C) Gas 7.

Peel apples and slice into saucepan. Add butter, caster sugar and water. Stew, uncovered, for about 15 minutes till apples are reduced to a purée and liquid has been absorbed. Leave to cool.

Roll out pastry on a lightly floured surface to ¼ inch (6mm) thickness. Cut out as many circles as you can, using a disc of cardboard or a saucer as a guide. Brush edges of pastry circles with a mixture of egg yolk and milk beaten lightly together.

Divide apple purée among the pastry circles, placing mixture in the centre. Fold pastry over and press edges together well. Use back of knife to knock up edges and mark them with a fork. Make decorative markings on top with a knife. Do not pierce pastry. Brush with remaining egg yolk and milk mixture.

Place on a lightly greased and floured baking tray and cook in the oven for 15–20 minutes. Serve hot.

French baked apples

Overall timing 1 hour 20 minutes

Freezing Not suitable

To serve 6

8 oz	**Mixed dried fruits**	**225 g**
1¼ pints	**Milk**	**700 ml**
10 oz	**White pudding rice**	**275 g**
3 tbsp	**Granulated sugar**	**3×15 ml**
	Pinch of salt	
6	**Bramley apples**	**6**
2 oz	**Butter**	**50 g**
6 tbsp	**Caster sugar**	**6×15 ml**
8 tbsp	**Raspberry jam**	**8×15 ml**

Preheat the oven to 375°F (190°C) Gas 5.

Just cover the dried fruits with water and cook, covered, for 25 minutes.

Boil the milk in a saucepan. Add the rice, granulated sugar and salt. Cover and simmer gently for about 30 minutes. Mix together rice and drained fruit.

Wash, dry and core apples. Place on a greased baking tray. Place a small knob of butter on each apple and sprinkle with 1 tbsp (15 ml) sugar. Bake for about 25 minutes on middle shelf of oven, or until apples are tender.

Heat, then sieve raspberry jam. Keep syrup warm. Divide rice mixture between 6 dishes, with apples on top. Serve with syrup.

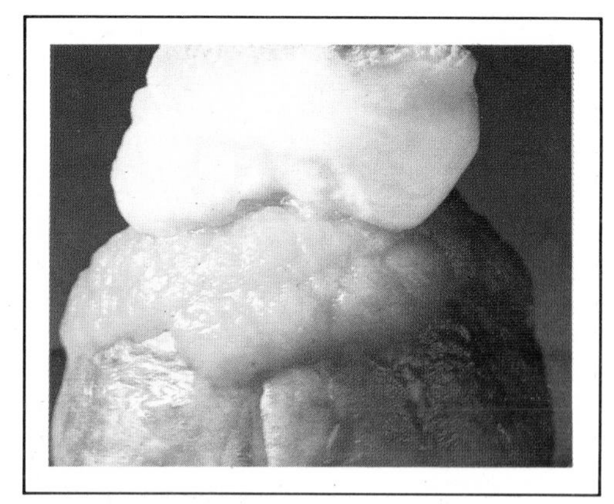

Norwegian baked apples

Overall timing 40 minutes

Freezing Not suitable

To serve 4

4	**Dessert apples**	**4**
1 oz	**Butter**	**25 g**
3 teasp	**Caster sugar**	**3×5 ml**
1	**Egg white**	**1**
8 tbsp	**Apple purée**	**8×15 ml**
1 tbsp	**Cointreau**	**15 ml**
1 oz	**Nibbed almonds**	**25 g**

Preheat the oven to 350°F (180°C) Gas 4.

Wash, dry and core apples. Place in an ovenproof dish. Dot with butter and sprinkle with sugar. Bake for 25 minutes.

Beat the egg white and remaining 1 teasp (5 ml) sugar until very stiff.

Fill apples with apple purée, pour some liqueur over and top with the whisked egg white.

Bake in the oven until golden brown. Decorate with almonds and serve hot.

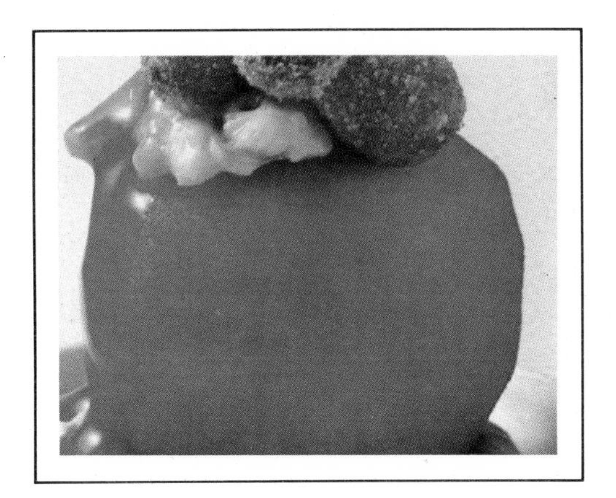

Bulgarian poached apples

Overall timing 13 minutes plus cooling

Freezing Not suitable

To serve 4		
1 tbsp	**Chopped almonds**	**15 ml**
1 tbsp	**Chopped hazelnuts**	**15 ml**
4	**Dessert apples**	**4**
¾ pint	**Red wine**	**400 ml**
3 oz	**Granulated sugar**	**75 g**
2 oz	**Black grapes**	**50 g**
¼ pint	**Cold, thick custard**	**150 ml**
4	**Jam tarts**	**4**
1 tbsp	**Redcurrant jelly**	**15 ml**
1 teasp	**Arrowroot**	**5 ml**
	Caster sugar	

Spread all nuts on a baking tray and grill for 5 minutes.

Peel and core apples. Poach gently in red wine, with sugar and a little water for about 8 minutes.

Meanwhile, halve half of the grapes and remove the seeds. Mix into custard with the almonds and hazelnuts.

Lift apples out and place each on a jam tart in individual serving dishes. Fill centres with custard mixture. Boil up apple liquid. Mix in redcurrant jelly and thicken with arrowroot.

Lightly dip the grapes in the sauce then roll them in sugar. Pour a little of the sauce over each apple and decorate with grapes. Leave to stand in cool place for 20 minutes.

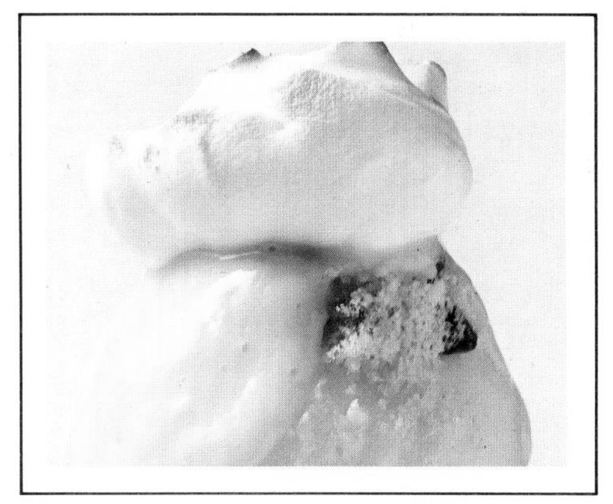

Meringue-topped apples

Overall timing 1 hour

Freezing Not suitable

To serve 6		
6	**Apples**	**6**
¼ pint	**Sweet white wine**	**150 ml**
3 tbsp	**Caster sugar**	**3×15 ml**
1	**Lemon**	**1**
1 tbsp	**Ground almonds**	**15 ml**
3 tbsp	**Currants**	**3×15 ml**
Custard		
1 tbsp	**Cornflour**	**15 ml**
½ pint	**Milk**	**300 ml**
1 tbsp	**Caster sugar**	**15 ml**
1 teasp	**Vanilla essence**	**5 ml**
2	**Egg yolks**	**2**
Topping		
2	**Egg whites**	**2**
2 tbsp	**Caster sugar**	**2×15 ml**

Peel and core the apples, but leave whole. Put the wine and 2 tbsp (2×15 ml) of sugar in pan. Finely grate lemon rind. Squeeze juice into pan. Add apples; poach 5 minutes.

Preheat oven to 350°F (180°C) Gas 4. Arrange apples in dish. Mix lemon rind, almonds, remaining sugar and currants. Divide between apple cavities. Blend cornflour with milk, sugar and vanilla. Bring to boil; simmer 3–4 minutes. Cool slightly; whisk in egg yolks. Pour over apples.

Whisk egg whites; whisk in sugar. Spoon over apples; bake 15 minutes. Serve hot.

Dartois

Overall timing 40 minutes plus thawing time for pastry

Freezing Not suitable

To serve 8

13 oz	Packet of frozen puff pastry	375 g
12 oz	Red Delicious apples	350 g
14 oz	Can of apple purée	410 g
1 oz	Sachet of vanilla sugar	25 g
1	Egg	1

Thaw pastry according to instructions on packet, then preheat oven to 425°F (220°C) Gas 7.

Peel and dice apples. Mix with apple purée and vanilla sugar.

Divide pastry into 2. Roll out each half on a lightly floured board to a rectangle about 9×12 inches (228×303mm) and 1/8 inch (3mm) thick.

Place one rectangle on a wetted baking tray. Spread apple mixture evenly on top, leaving a 1 1/4 inch (3cm) border all the way round. Wet pastry edges slightly. Cover with second rectangle and press edges together well. Using the back of knife, lightly run diagonal lines across pastry top to give lattice effect. Be careful not to pierce pastry. Knock up pastry edges and flute, using the back of a knife.

Beat the egg and brush over pastry. Cook for 5 minutes in the oven. Reduce heat to 400°F (200°C) Gas 6 and cook for a further 25 minutes. Reglaze during baking so the pastry becomes a deep golden colour.

Cut Dartois into slices and serve as soon as possible after cooking, before the pastry loses its "puff". As with all apple pastry desserts, a serving of thick whipped cream with each slice makes a delicious extra.

Tarte sucrée aux pommes

Overall timing 1 hour plus thawing

Freezing Not suitable

To serve 6–8

13 oz	Packet of frozen puff pastry	375g
2 lb	Dessert apples	900 g
2 tbsp	Lemon juice	2×15 ml
5 oz	Caster sugar	150 g
3 oz	Sultanas	75 g
2 teasp	Ground cinnamon	2×5 ml

Thaw pastry. Preheat oven to 375°F (190°C) Gas 5.

Peel and core the apples and cut into thin slices. Place in a bowl with lemon juice and 3 oz (75 g) of the caster sugar and toss lightly.

Roll out the pastry to a 14×6 inch (35×15cm) rectangle. Place on wetted baking tray, knock up and crimp the edges. Prick along the centre with a fork. Arrange the apple slices in lines along the length of the pastry, overlapping them as they shrink during cooking.

Sprinkle with sultanas and any remaining sugar in bowl from apples. Bake in the centre of the oven for 40 minutes.

Remove from oven and sprinkle with the remaining sugar mixed with the cinnamon. Cut into slices and serve hot or cold with whipped or pouring cream.

Variations

Other fruits which could be used are apricots (halve, remove stones, then arrange cut side up) and Williams pears (prepare as apples).

Cherry rice ring

Overall timing 45 minutes

Freezing Not suitable

To serve 6–8

8 oz	**Long grain rice**	**225 g**
4fl oz	**Water**	**120 ml**
3 oz	**Granulated sugar**	**75 g**
4 tbsp	**Apple juice**	**4×15 ml**
4 tbsp	**Single cream**	**4×15 ml**
1½ lb	**Can of cherries**	**700 g**
1	**Lemon**	**1**
2 tbsp	**Arrowroot**	**2×15 ml**
3 tbsp	**Lemon juice**	**3×15 ml**
6 tbsp	**Caster sugar**	**6×15 ml**
	Red food colouring	

Cook rice in boiling water 10 minutes. Drain; rinse well.

Put measured water, sugar and apple juice in a pan. Boil, stirring to dissolve sugar. Add rice, boil again; cover and cook slowly 15 minutes until liquid is absorbed and rice cooked. Stir in cream. Remove from heat; keep covered.

Drain cherries; reserve juice. Heat cherries and 6 tbsp (6×15 ml) reserved juice. Remove a third of cherries; mix into rice.

Oil a 1½ pint (850 ml) ring mould and fill with rice. Press down well, invert on to a warm plate. Keep mould in place so rice stays hot. Grate rind from lemon: squeeze.

Bring cherries to the boil. Blend 1 tbsp (15 ml) of arrowroot with 2 tbsp (2×15 ml) of reserved cherry juice, lemon juice and 2 tbsp (2×15 ml) caster sugar; stir into cherries. Add lemon rind, bring to boil; add few drops of colouring. Pour into centre of ring. Keep warm.

Make remaining juice up to ½ pint (300 ml) with leftover lemon juice, or water. Blend 2 teasp (2×5 ml) arrowroot with remaining sugar and juice to make a thin paste. Bring juice to boil; stir into paste.

Return to pan, stir over medium heat till sauce clears and thickens. Add a little colouring. Serve hot.

Grape and apple tart

Overall timing 1 hour plus pastry preparation time

Freezing Suitable

To serve 6

Sweet flan pastry

6 oz	Plain flour	175 g
3 oz	Caster sugar	75 g
	Salt	
3½ oz	Softened butter	100 g
2	Egg yolks	2
Filling		
2 oz	Caster sugar	50 g
8 oz	White grapes	225 g
4	Medium-sized cooking apples	4
3 tbsp	Apricot jam	3×15 ml
1 tbsp	Water	15 ml

To make pastry, place flour, sugar, pinch of salt and butter, cut into small pieces, in a large bowl. Work the mixture between the fingers and palms of your hands until mixture resembles fine crumbs.

Add egg yolks and work them into the mixture very quickly with your hand. When the pastry no longer sticks to your fingers, shape it into a ball, wrap and place in fridge for 1 hour.

Preheat the oven to 400°F (200°C) Gas 6. Roll out pastry and use to line a 9 inch (23cm) flan ring, placed on a baking tray. Prick the base with a fork, sprinkle with sugar and bake for 10 minutes.

Meanwhile, wash and drain the grapes. Peel apples and cut them in half. Remove cores, cut each half almost in to slices, without separating them at the base. Remove flan from oven.

Place jam and water in saucepan and cook gently until runny. Arrange halved apples, flat side down, on base of the flan, surround with grapes and brush with jam. Cook in oven for 20–25 minutes, until apples are golden. Serve warm or cold.

Krapfen

Overall timing 40 minutes

Freezing Not suitable

Makes about 20

2	Eggs	2
3fl oz	Beer	90 ml
4 oz	Plain flour	125 g
	Pinch of salt	
1½ lb	Dessert apples	700 g
	Oil for frying	
	Caster sugar	
	Cinnamon	

Separate the eggs. Put the yolks, beer, flour and salt into a bowl and beat to a smooth batter. In another bowl, beat the egg whites till stiff then fold into the batter.

Peel and grate apples then mix them into the batter.

Heat oil for frying to 360°F (180°C) in a deep fryer.

Slide spoonfuls of the apple and batter mixture into the hot oil and fry for about 5 minutes or until crisp. Turn them over once during cooking.

When cooked, remove from pan with a draining spoon and drain on kitchen paper. Roll krapfen in caster sugar, or caster sugar and cinnamon mixed together. Serve hot.

Canadian apple pie

Overall timing 1 hour

Freezing Suitable

To serve 8

12 oz	Shortcrust pastry	350 g
Filling		
6	Dessert apples	6
3 oz	Light muscovado sugar	75 g
1 oz	Granulated sugar	25 g
1 teasp	Ground cinnamon	5 ml
¼ teasp	Grated nutmeg	1.25 ml
½ pint	Double cream	284 ml
1	Egg yolk	1

Preheat the oven to 425°F (220°C) Gas 7. Roll out two-thirds of the pastry on a lightly floured surface and use to line a 9 inch (23cm) pie dish. Prick the base with a fork.

Peel, core and chop the apples. Place in a bowl with the sugars and spices. Add the cream and mix lightly. Pour into the pie dish.

Roll out the remaining pastry and use to cover the filling. Crimp the edges, using the point of a knife to make a decorative pattern. Prick the top of the pie and brush with lightly beaten egg yolk.

Bake in the centre of the oven for 15 minutes, then reduce the heat to 400°F (200°C) Gas 6 and cook for a further 30 minutes till golden. Serve hot or cold.

Alsatian apple tart

Overall timing 1½ hours including chilling

Freezing Not suitable

To serve 6–8		
Pastry		
8 oz	**Plain flour**	**225 g**
4 oz	**Butter**	**125 g**
2 tbsp	**Caster sugar**	**2×15 ml**
1	**Egg**	**1**
	White wine to mix	
Filling		
4	**Golden Delicious apples**	**4**
1 tbsp	**Caster sugar**	**15 ml**
½ pint	**Double cream**	**284 ml**
2	**Eggs**	**2**
2	**Sachets of vanilla sugar**	**2**
1	**Lemon**	**1**
2 oz	**Caster sugar**	**50 g**

Put flour into a bowl, add butter, cut in pieces: rub in till mixture resembles crumbs. Stir in sugar. Add egg yolk and enough white wine to form a firm dough. Chill 30 minutes.

Preheat oven to 400°F (200°C) Gas 6.

Roll out pastry and use to line a 9 inch (23cm) flan dish. Place on a baking tray, line pastry with foil and fill with baking beans. Bake near top of oven 20 minutes.

Peel apples, cut in half and remove cores. Arrange on pastry, rounded side up; sprinkle with sugar. Bake 10 minutes in centre of oven. Whip cream, beat in eggs, vanilla sugar, grated rind of lemon and sugar till creamy. Spread over apples. Reduce heat to 350°F (180°C) Gas 4 and cook for 20 minutes. Serve hot.

Pineapple upside-down pudding

Overall timing 1½ hours

Freezing Suitable: bake in 375°F (190°C) Gas 5 oven for 1½–2 hours

To serve 6–8

Topping		
2 oz	Butter	50 g
3 tbsp	Soft brown sugar	3×15 ml
8	Canned pineapple rings	8
	Glacé cherries	
Sponge		
6 oz	Butter or margarine	175 g
6 oz	Caster sugar	175 g
3	Eggs	3
9 oz	Self-raising flour	250 g
	Grated rind of 1 lemon	
4 tbsp	Milk	4×15 ml

Preheat the oven to 350°F (180°C) Gas 4. Grease and base-line an 8 inch (20cm) spring-form tin.

To make the topping, cream together the butter and brown sugar and spread over the bottom of the tin. Place one of the pineapple rings in the centre and surround with the remaining rings, halved. Decorate with halved glacé cherries, cut sides up.

To make the sponge, cream the fat and sugar together in a bowl till pale and fluffy. Add the eggs one at a time, beating well between each addition. Beat in the sifted flour and the lemon rind, adding the milk to give a soft dropping consistency.

Spread carefully over the pineapple and smooth the top. Bake in the centre of the oven for about 1 hour, till the sponge is firm and springy to the touch.

Invert the tin on to a warmed serving dish and remove the sides and base carefully. Decorate with extra glacé cherries, if liked, and serve immediately with pouring cream or hot custard.

Banana pudding with rum sauce

Overall timing 1¼ hours

Freezing Suitable: reheat in 350°F (180°C) Gas 4 oven

To serve 6

2 lb	Bananas	900 g
3½ oz	Caster sugar	100 g
2 oz	Softened butter	50 g
2 oz	Plain flour	50 g
	Grated nutmeg	
2	Eggs	2
2 tbsp	Icing sugar	2×15 ml
1 tbsp	Rum or rum flavouring	15 ml
¼ pint	Carton of single cream	150 ml

Preheat the oven to 350°F (180°C) Gas 4.

Reserve half a large or 1 medium-sized banana for decoration. Peel the rest. Mash them with a fork in a bowl with sugar, butter, flour and a pinch of nutmeg.

Separate the eggs. Add yolks to banana mixture and beat well with a wooden spoon until smooth and creamy. Beat the egg whites till very stiff, then gently fold into the banana mixture.

Lightly grease and flour a pudding basin. Fill with the banana mixture and bake for 1 hour.

Remove from oven. Leave to cool slightly then turn out on a warmed serving plate. Sprinkle with icing sugar and decorate with the reserved banana, sliced. Mix rum or rum flavouring into cream and serve separately.

Apple and mincemeat tart

Overall timing 1 hour

Freezing Suitable: reheat in 350°F (180°C) Gas 4 oven for 40 minutes

To serve 6

8 oz	Shortcrust pastry (see Canadian apple pie, page 24)	225 g
14½ oz	Jar of mincemeat	411 g
1 lb	Bramley apples	450 g
3 oz	Caster sugar	75 g
½ teasp	Ground allspice	2.5 ml
2 oz	Butter	50 g
1 tbsp	Plain flour	15 ml

Preheat the oven to 425°F (220°C) Gas 7. Roll out the dough and line a 9½ inch (24cm) fluted loose-bottomed flan tin. Spread mincemeat evenly over pastry.

Peel, core and finely slice the apples. Mix with 2 oz (50 g) of sugar and the allspice. Arrange in circles on mincemeat.

In a bowl, cut and fold the butter with remaining 1 oz (25 g) sugar and flour until the mixture resembles fine breadcrumbs. Sprinkle evenly over the apples. Place flan on a baking tray.

Bake in oven for 15 minutes, then reduce to 375°F (190°C) Gas 5 and bake for a further 30 minutes. Remove from oven and allow to cool.

Lift tart from flan tin and place on serving plate. Spoon any topping from baking tray on to tart. Serve warm or cold, with whipped cream or vanilla ice cream.

Russian pudding

Overall timing 30 minutes

Freezing Not suitable

To serve 4–6

1½ pints	Milk	850 ml
	Pinch of salt	
	Grated rind of ½ lemon	
4 oz	Granulated sugar	125 g
3 oz	Semolina or ground rice	75 g
1	Egg	1
1 lb	Can of cherries	453 g
2 tbsp	Redcurrent jelly	2×15 ml

In a saucepan, heat the milk, salt, lemon rind and 2 oz (50 g) of the sugar. Stir in the semolina or ground rice. Remove from the heat.

Separate the egg and add the beaten yolk to the saucepan.

In a bowl, beat the egg white till stiff and carefully fold into the semolina or ground rice mixture.

Drain cherries. Place cherries and 2 tbsp (2×15 ml) of the juice in a pan. Stir in the redcurrent jelly and cook for 5 minutes.

Preheat the grill. Grease a flameproof serving dish. Pour in half the semolina or rice mixture, then all the cherry mixture and finally the rest of the semolina or rice. Sprinkle with the remaining sugar and place under the grill. Cook till the sugar caramelizes and turns golden but not brown – it should take about 3 minutes. Serve immediately.

Apple and marmalade charlotte

Overall timing 1 hour

Freezing Suitable: reheat in 400°F (200°C) Gas 6 oven for 10 minutes

To serve 8

2½ lb	**Cooking apples**	**1.1 kg**
4 tbsp	**Water**	**4×15 ml**
1 oz	**Sugar**	**25 g**
4 oz	**Marmalade**	**125 g**
1½ lb	**Stale sliced bread**	**700 g**
3 oz	**Butter**	**75 g**

Preheat oven to 400°F (200°C) Gas 6.

To make the filling, peel apples, core and slice into a large saucepan. Add water, cover and bring to the boil. Cook over medium heat for 12 minutes without removing the lid at all during cooking. Remove from heat and beat in sugar and marmalade with a wooden spoon.

Remove crusts and butter bread. Cut a third of slices into triangles, and the rest into wide fingers.

Grease a 3 pint (1.7 litre) charlotte mould and line the bottom with some of the bread triangles, buttered-side out. Overlap the slices as the bread tends to shrink during cooking. Line sides of mould with over-lapping bread fingers, butter-side out.

Pour in apple mixture and top with remaining bread triangles, butter-side up. Cook on centre shelf of the oven for 30–40 minutes till golden brown.

Remove from oven. Leave to cool slightly in the mould. Run a knife around the edge and turn out on to a warmed serving plate. Serve hot with custard or cream.

Cold pies, puddings and desserts

Lemon meringue pie

Overall timing 40–45 minutes plus chilling

Freezing Not suitable

To serve 6		
Pastry		
4 oz	**Plain flour**	**125 g**
	Pinch of salt	
2 oz	**Butter or margarine**	**50 g**
4 teasp	**Cold water**	**4×5 ml**
Filling		
3 tbsp	**Cornflour**	**3×15 ml**
¼ pint	**Water**	**150 ml**
2	**Large lemons**	**2**
4 oz	**Granulated sugar**	**125 g**
2	**Large eggs**	**2**
3 oz	**Caster sugar**	**75 g**

To make pastry, sift flour and salt into a bowl. Add butter or margarine, cut into pieces, and rub in till mixture resembles fine crumbs. Stir in the water and mix to form a dough. Roll dough into a ball, wrap and chill for 15 minutes.

Preheat the oven to 425°F (220°C) Gas 7.

Roll out pastry and use to line a 7 inch (17.5 cm) flan case or deep pie plate. Trim and fill with foil and baking beans and bake blind for 15 minutes. Remove foil and beans and cook for further 5 minutes.

Meanwhile to make filling, blend cornflour with the water in a pan. Add the finely grated lemon rinds and juice to pan and bring slowly to the boil, stirring constantly. Simmer for 2 minutes, stirring. Remove from heat.

Stir in the granulated sugar and leave to cool slightly. Separate the eggs and beat the yolks into the cornflour mixture. Pour the mixture into the prepared flan case.

Stiffly whisk the egg whites, add half the sugar and whisk again till thick and glossy then fold in the remaining sugar lightly. Put meringue into a forcing bag fitted with a star nozzle and pipe meringue over surface of filling to enclose it completely.

Bake in centre of oven for 10 minutes till meringue is lightly golden.

Savarin au chocolat

Overall timing 1½ hours

Freezing Suitable

To serve 4–6

2 oz	Plain chocolate cake covering	50 g
1½ pints	Milk	850 ml
6 oz	Caster sugar	175 g
16	Sponge fingers	16
1 tbsp	Kirsch or brandy	15 ml
3	Eggs	3
¼ teasp	Vanilla essence	1.25 ml
3 tbsp	Water	3×15 ml
¼ pint	Carton of double cream	150 ml
10	Glacé cherries	10

Grate the chocolate very finely and add to the milk in a saucepan. Cook, stirring, over very gentle heat till just boiling. Add 3 oz (75 g) of the sugar and the sponge fingers, broken up. Cook gently for 30 minutes, stirring frequently with a wooden spoon. Push through sieve into bowl, stir in the Kirsch or brandy and leave to cool.

Preheat oven to 425°F (220°C) Gas 7. Beat the eggs with the vanilla and add to the cool mixture. Caramelize the remainder of the sugar with the water in a saucepan and use to coat base of a 2½ pint (1.1 litre) ring mould.

Pour in the chocolate mixture and bake in the centre of the oven for about 40 minutes or until set. Remove from oven and leave to cool completely. Run knife round edge, turn out and decorate with whipped cream and cherries.

Chocolate and sesame tart

Overall timing 50 minutes plus chilling

Freezing Not suitable

To serve 6

8 oz	Shortcrust pastry (see Canadian apple pie, page 24)	225 g
3½ oz	Plain dessert chocolate	100 g
2	Egg yolks	2
¼ pint	Carton of whipping cream	150 ml
3 tbsp	Caster sugar	3×15 ml
4 teasp	Sesame seeds	4×5 ml

Preheat the oven to 400°F (200°C) Gas 6. Lightly grease an 8 inch (20cm) flan tin.

Roll out the pastry and use to line the flan tin. Trim and crimp the edges. Prick the base, line with foil and spread with baking beans. Bake blind for 20 minutes.

Remove the foil and beans, then bake for a further 5–10 minutes still crisp. Leave to cool completely.

Break the chocolate into pieces and put into a bowl over a pan of simmering water. Stir over a low heat till melted and smooth. Remove from the heat and stir in the egg yolks one at a time. Leave to cool.

Whip the cream till soft peaks form, fold in the sugar. Fold into the chocolate. Spread the mixture into the cold pastry case and smooth the top. Chill for 1 hour.

Meanwhile, spread sesame seeds on a baking tray and grill till golden brown. Leave to cool completely.

Remove the flan from tin and place on a serving dish. Sprinkle with the toasted sesame seeds and serve immediately with pouring cream.

Tarte aux poires

Overall timing 1¾ hours plus chilling

Freezing Not suitable

To serve 6–8

Hazelnut pastry		
8 oz	Plain flour	225 g
4 oz	Butter or margarine	125 g
2 oz	Ground hazelnuts	50 g
1 tbsp	Caster sugar	15 ml
2	Egg yolks	2
2 tbsp	Cold water	2×15 ml
Filling		
1½ lb	Firm pears	700 g
¼ pint	Water	150 ml
2 oz	Caster sugar	50 g
Crème pâtissière		
1 pint	Milk	560 ml
1	Strip of lemon rind	1
8 tbsp	Caster sugar	8×15 ml
4	Medium eggs	4
4 tbsp	Plain flour	4×15 ml

Additional ingredients		
4 oz	Strawberry jam	125 g

Make pastry: sift flour. Rub in fat. Stir in nuts and sugar; add egg yolks and water. Mix to form a soft dough. Chill 30 minutes.

Peel, quarter and core pears. Put water and sugar in pan; heat gently till sugar dissolves. Add pears; simmer 10 minutes till just tender. Drain pears, reserving syrup.

Preheat oven to 400°F (200°C) Gas 6 and heat baking tray. Roll out pastry and line a 9 inch (23cm) flan dish. Prick base with fork, line with foil and baking beans. Stand dish on hot tray; bake 25–30 minutes.

Make the crème pâtissière: put milk and lemon rind in a pan and bring to boil. Infuse, off heat, 10 minutes; remove lemon rind. Beat sugar and eggs in a bowl, stir in flour then milk; strain into pan and slowly bring to boil. Cook, stirring 2–4 minutes until thick. Pour into cooled flan case; leave to set.

Add jam to syrup; boil till thick enough to coat back of spoon; sieve. Arrange pears in flan and spoon over glaze. Serve cold.

Apple and almond flan

Overall timing 1 hour plus chilling

Freezing Not suitable

Cuts into 8

7 oz	Plain flour	200 g
	Pinch of salt	
5 oz	Butter	150 g
2 tbsp	Caster sugar	2×15 ml
2 tbsp	Cold water	2×15 ml
1 lb	Can of apple purée	450 g
1 lb	Dessert apples	450 g
4 tbsp	Apricot jam	4×15 ml
3 tbsp	Apricot brandy or Curaçao	3×15 ml
2 oz	Nibbed almonds	50 g

Sift the flour and salt into a bowl. Rub in the butter till the mixture resembles fine breadcrumbs. Stir in the sugar. Add the water, stirring, and knead into a smooth ball.

Roll out the pastry on a floured surface and use to line base and sides of a greased 8 inch (20cm) springform tin. Place in the fridge for 30 minutes.

Preheat the oven to 425°F (220°C) Gas 7. Place baking tray in oven to heat.

Spread apple purée over base of flan. Peel, core and thickly slice the apples. Arrange the slices in overlapping circles on top of the filling. Warm the jam and brandy together till smooth and brush over the apple slices. Sprinkle the almonds around the edge and over the centre.

Place the tin on a baking tray and bake in the centre of the oven for 30 minutes. Remove from the oven and leave to cool completely. Remove from the springform tin, place on a serving dish and serve with whipped cream.

Pears in red wine

Overall timing 1¼ hours plus chilling

Freezing Not suitable

To serve 8

1	Orange	1
8 oz	Caster sugar	225 g
½ pint	Claret or Burgundy	300 ml
½ pint	Water	300 ml
2 inch	Cinnamon stick	5cm
8	Ripe pears	8

Preheat the oven to 350°F (180°C) Gas 4.

Wash the orange and thinly pare away the rind with a potato peeler. Shred the rind finely and put into a deep, flameproof casserole. Add the sugar, wine and water and heat gently, stirring till the sugar dissolves. Add the cinnamon stick and boil for 2 minutes. Remove from the heat.

Peel the pears, leaving the stalks on, and stand them in the red wine syrup. Cover the dish with a large piece of foil, pushing the stalks through the foil to hold the pears upright.

Bake in the centre of the oven for about 25 minutes, till the pears are tender. Remove from the syrup and arrange in a serving dish.

Boil the syrup rapidly till reduced by half. Remove the cinnamon stick and spoon the sauce over the pears. Leave to cool, then chill for 2–3 hours, basting the syrup over the pears occasionally.

Serve with whipped cream and sponge fingers.

Chocolate profiteroles

Overall timing 1½ hours

Freezing Suitable: filling and sauce

To serve 4–6		
4 oz	**Plain flour**	**125 g**
8fl oz	**Water**	**220 ml**
3 oz	**Unsalted butter**	**75 g**
¼ teasp	**Salt**	**1.25 ml**
3	**Eggs**	**3**
1 pint	**Whipping cream**	**600 ml**
Chocolate sauce		
6 oz	**Plain chocolate**	**175 g**
1 oz	**Butter**	**25 g**

Preheat the oven to 425°F (220°C) Gas 7.

Sift flour. Put water, butter and salt into saucepan and bring to boil, stirring to melt butter. Remove from heat and beat in flour all at once. Return to heat and beat till dough pulls away from sides of pan. Gradually beat in eggs to make a soft, glossy dough.

Using a teaspoon, drop paste in balls on to greased baking trays, easing them off with a second teaspoon. Bake for 20–25 minutes till golden and crisp. Transfer to a wire rack. Make a slit in each bun to release steam. Cool.

Whip cream and use to fill buns. Pile on a serving plate.

To make sauce, melt chocolate with butter and 2 tbsp (2×15 ml) water in a bowl over a pan of hot water. Cool slightly, then pour over choux buns.

Rice and apricot condé

Overall timing 1¼ hours plus chilling

Freezing Not suitable

To serve 6–8

5 oz	Short grain rice	150 g
1¾ pint	Milk	1 litre
2× 14.8 oz	Cans of apricot halves	2×420 g
1	Vanilla pod	1
3 oz	Caster sugar	75 g
2 oz	Butter	50 g
3	Egg yolks	3
	Bland oil	
	Glacé cherries	
	Angelica	

Wash the rice. Put the milk into a saucepan and bring to the boil. Stir in the rice, cover and simmer for about 40 minutes till tender, stirring occasionally.

Meanwhile, put the apricots and juice in a saucepan. Add the vanilla pod, bring to the boil and simmer for 5 minutes. Remove from heat and leave to cool.

Remove rice from the heat and stir in the sugar and butter. Beat in the egg yolks.

Lightly oil a 3 pint (1.7 litre) ring mould and pour rice mixture into it. Smooth top and leave to cool. Chill for 3–4 hours.

Turn rice mould out on to a serving dish. Remove apricots from the syrup with a draining spoon and arrange in the centre and around the sides of the moulded rice.

Decorate with glacé cherries and angelica and spoon the syrup over, first removing the vanilla pod.

Creamy liqueur mould

Overall timing 10 minutes plus chilling

Freezing Not suitable

To serve 4

3 tbsp	Cornflour	3×15 ml
4 tbsp	Water	4×15 ml
1	Large can of evaporated milk	1
2 tbsp	Grand Marnier or Curaçao	2×15 ml
	Caster sugar	

Mix the cornflour and water in a bowl until smooth.

In a saucepan heat the evaporated milk and stir in the cornflour mixture. Bring to the boil and cook, stirring, until thickened. Remove from heat, add liqueur and sweeten to taste with caster sugar.

Rinse a 1 pint (560 ml) mould with cold water, then pour in the mixture and when cool place in fridge. Chill till set.

To unmould, dip up to rim in hot water for a few seconds, then invert on to a serving plate. Serve with fresh or stewed fruit.

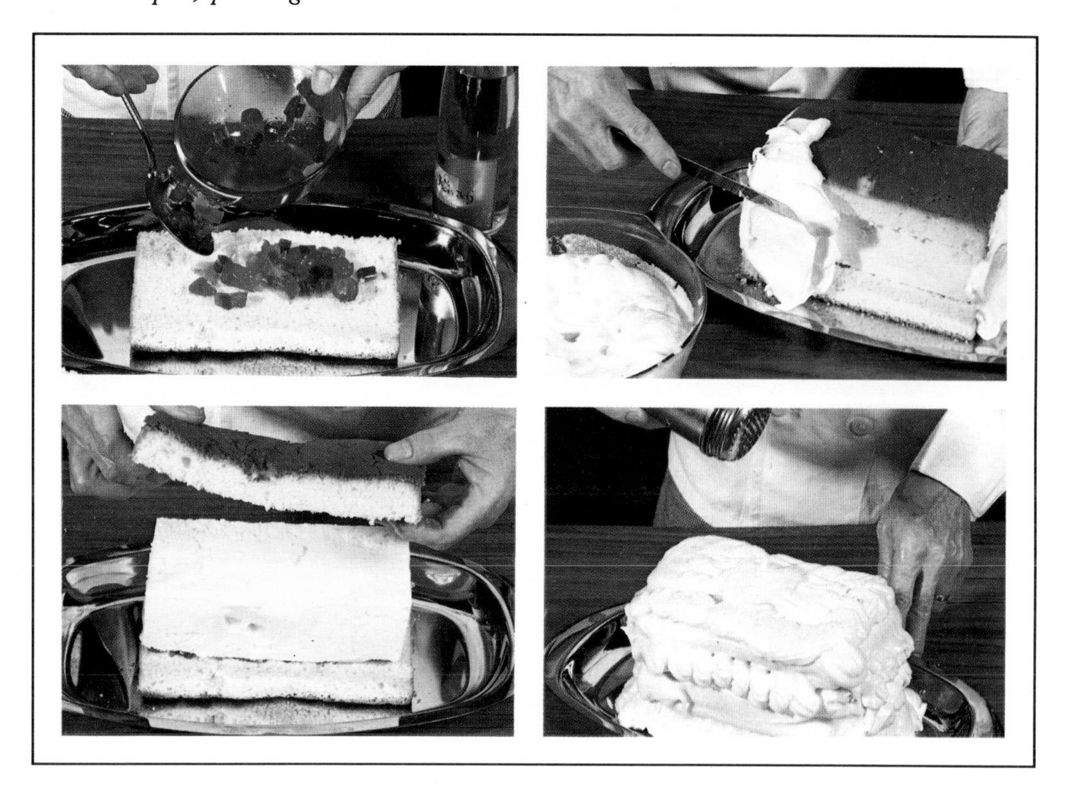

Baked Alaska

Overall timing 30 minutes plus 1 hour marination

Freezing Not suitable

To serve 6

4 oz	Glacé fruit	125 g
4 tbsp	Kirsch or other liqueur	4×15 ml
6	Egg whites	6
12 oz	Icing sugar	350 g
	Pinch of cream of tartar	
	Pinch of salt	
1 tbsp	Lemon juice	15 ml
1	Sponge cake	1
1 pint	Block of vanilla ice cream	560 ml

Put glacé fruit and liqueur in a bowl and chill for 1 hour.

Preheat the oven to 475°F (240°C) Gas 9.

Put egg whites, sifted icing sugar, cream of tartar, salt and lemon juice in a bowl placed over a pan of hot water. Whisk over a very gentle heat till stiff and dry.

Cut sponge cake in half lengthways. Place 1 layer on baking tray. Spoon fruit and liqueur over, then put ice cream on top. Cover with the other sponge layer.

Working quickly, pipe or spread whisked white all over cake, making sure all the ice cream is covered.

Dredge with a little icing sugar and bake in hot oven for 5 minutes or until meringue is golden. Serve immediately.

Empress pudding

Overall timing 1½ hours plus chilling

Freezing Not suitable

To serve 6		
2 oz	Chopped angelica	50 g
2 oz	Glacé cherries	50 g
2 tbsp	Kirsch	2×15 ml
6 oz	Long grain rice	175 g
1¼ pints	Milk	700 ml
	Salt	
4 oz	Caster sugar	125 g
Custard		
½ pint	Milk	300 ml
4 oz	Caster sugar	125 g
	Salt	
4	Egg yolks	4
¼ teasp	Vanilla essence	1.25 ml
1 tbsp	Powdered gelatine	15 ml
¼ pint	Whipping cream	150 ml

Soak angelica and cherries in Kirsch.

Wash rice in a sieve. Put in a saucepan, just cover with water, bring to the boil and simmer for 5 minutes, then drain and return to saucepan. Bring the milk to the boil in a saucepan and at once add to the rice with a pinch of salt. Half cover the pan and cook gently for about 20 minutes. Add the caster sugar and cook gently for 25 minutes or until the milk is absorbed.

To make the custard, bring the milk to the boil with the sugar and a pinch of salt. Put egg yolks into a bowl, pour a little of the milk over and mix well. Return to pan, add the vanilla essence and continue to stir till the custard thickens slightly. Do not boil.

Mix gelatine with 3 tbsp (3×15 ml) water. Melt over a pan of hot water, then whisk into the custard mixture. Add the rice mixture, angelica and fruit with the Kirsch to the custard and allow to cool.

Whisk the cream until it holds stiff peaks, then stir into the rice mixture. Pour into a wetted mould and leave to set in the fridge for about 3 hours.

To serve, quickly dip mould in hot water and turn out on to a plate.

Mille-feuilles de val de loire

Overall timing 30 minutes plus thawing

Freezing Not suitable

To serve 6

13 oz	**Packet of frozen puff pastry**	**375 g**
1 tbsp	**Kirsch**	**15 ml**
6 oz	**Raspberry jam**	**175 g**

Thaw pastry. Preheat the oven to 425°F (220°C) Gas 6.

Roll out the pastry to a 12 inch (30cm) square. Cut into 3 even sized rectangles, trim edges and knock up. Place on a wetted baking tray, prick several times with a fork. Mark one of the rectangles into six 2 inch (5cm) wide slices with a sharp knife.

Bake for about 10 minutes till well risen and golden, then transfer to a wire rack and cool.

Place one of the unmarked rectangles on a flat board. Mix together the Kirsch and jam and spread a third of it evenly over the pastry. Cover with the other unmarked rectangle, spread another third of the jam over, then cover with the marked rectangle and top with remaining jam or white glacé icing*.

Cut into slices along marked lines. If liked, serve with whipped cream or pouring cream.

*To make white glacé icing, blend 4 oz (125 g) sifted icing sugar with 1–2 tbsp (1–2×15 ml) hot water. The icing should be thick enough to coat the back of a spoon. If too thick add more water, if too runny, add more icing sugar.

Chocolate meringue cups

Overall timing 15 minutes plus meringue preparation time

Freezing Not suitable

To serve 6

5 oz	**Plain chocolate**	**150 g**
1 oz	**Butter or margarine**	**25 g**
9 tbsp	**Very strong dissolved instant coffee**	**9×15 ml**
½ pint	**Carton of double cream**	**300 ml**
1½ tbsp	**Icing sugar**	**1½× 15 ml**
36	**Small meringues (home-made or bought)**	**36**

Put the chocolate, broken into small pieces, in a small saucepan. Add the butter or margarine and the coffee and heat gently, stirring constantly, until the chocolate is melted. Keep sauce warm in the top of a double boiler.

Whip the cream until stiff and stir in the icing sugar. Place 4 meringues in each serving dish and pour over ¾ of the chocolate sauce. Add 2 more meringues to each dish then cover with the whipped cream and drizzle over the remaining chocolate sauce.

Banana split

Overall timing 5–8 minutes

Freezing Not suitable

To serve 1

2 oz	Plain chocolate	50 g
2-3 tbsp	Milk	2-3×15 ml
1	Banana	1
1	Scoop each of vanilla, chocolate and strawberry ice cream	1
	Whipped cream	
2 tbsp	Chopped walnuts	2×15 ml

Put the chocolate, broken into small pieces, in a bowl over a pan of hot water. Add the milk and heat until melted, stirring.

Peel and halve the banana lengthways and place the halves along the edge of a small oval serving dish.

Place the scoops of ice cream along the centre and spoon over the chocolate sauce.

Decorate with piped whipped cream and sprinkle with chopped walnuts. Serve immediately.

Albert's favourite trifle

Overall timing 1½ hours including chilling time

Freezing Not suitable

To serve 6–8

1 pint	**Milk**	**560 ml**
3 tbsp	**Custard powder**	**3×15 ml**
2 tbsp	**Sugar**	**2×15 ml**
6 oz	**Leftover sponge cake**	**175 g**
2 tbsp	**Raspberry jam**	**2×15 ml**
6 tbsp	**Sherry**	**6×15 ml**
1 lb 13 oz	**Can of sliced peaches**	**822 g**
¼ pint	**Carton of double or whipping cream**	**150 ml**
1 oz	**Toasted split almonds**	**25 g**

Blend 6 tbsp (6×15 ml) of the milk with the custard powder and sugar. Bring remaining milk to the boil, then pour on to powder and stir well. Return to pan and bring back to the boil, stirring continuously. Put to one side to cool, covering surface with wet greaseproof to prevent a skin forming.

Cut sponge into small pieces and spread with jam. Arrange around the base and sides of serving dish.

Drain peaches. Mix 3 tbsp (3×15 ml) of syrup from can with the sherry and sprinkle over the sponge. Reserve a few peaches for decoration and arrange the rest on top of sponge.

Remove greaseproof paper and beat cooled custard well. Pour over fruit and chill for 1 hour.

Whip cream until still then pipe on to trifle. Decorate with reserved peaches and sprinkle with toasted almonds.

Custard tart

Overall timing 1½ hours plus cooling

Freezing Not suitable

To serve 4–6

8 oz	Plain flour	225 g
2 oz	Lard	50 g
2 oz	Butter	50 g
2-3 tbsp	Water	2-3×15 ml
Filling		
1 pint	Milk	560 ml
1	Vanilla pod	1
	Strip of lemon rind	
4	Eggs	4
2 oz	Caster sugar	50 g
	Grated nutmeg	

Preheat the oven to 400°F (200°C) Gas 6.

Put the flour into a bowl and rub in the fat till the mixture resembles fine breadcrumbs. Gradually add the water and mix to a smooth dough.

Roll out the dough on a lightly floured surface and use to line a 9 inch (23 cm) flan tin or ring. Bake blind for 10 minutes. Remove from oven and reduce temperature to 350°F (180°C) Gas 4.

Put milk, vanilla pod and lemon rind into a pan and bring almost to the boil. Remove from heat and leave to infuse for 10 minutes. Remove vanilla pod and lemon rind.

Beat eggs and sugar in bowl. Pour in milk, stirring. Strain into flan case and sprinkle with nutmeg. Bake for 35 minutes or till just set. Cool.

Mille-Feuille

Overall timing 50–55 minutes plus pastry preparation time

Freezing Not suitable

To serve 6

1½ lb	**Puff pastry (see page 10, Galette des rois) or use frozen puff pastry**	700 g
4	**Egg yolks**	4
4 tbsp	**Caster sugar**	4×15 ml
1	**Small glass Marsala**	1
	Icing sugar	

To make puff pastry, see page 10 (and double the quantities given in Galette des rois). Preheat to the oven to 425°F (220°C) Gas 7.

Roll out pastry very thinly and cut into 4 rectangles about 7×13 inches (17.5×33cm). Lay the pastry on dampened baking trays and prick all over with a fork.

Bake for 10–15 minutes until golden brown and crisp. Remove from oven and leave to cool.

Meanwhile to prepare the custard, place egg yolks and caster sugar in a bowl and, using a wooden spoon, beat well for about 15 minutes then stir in the Marsala, a little at a time. Cook the custard over a gentle heat, stirring constantly, until it thickens, but do not allow mixture to boil. Leave to cool.

Put one rectangle of pastry on a serving dish and cover with a little of the custard. Continue layering the rectangles of pastry and custard in this way, finishing with a pastry layer. Dust liberally with icing sugar before serving.

Pineapple tartlets

Overall timing 2 hours

Freezing Not suitable

To serve 15

Pastry		
1 oz	Icing sugar	25 g
6 oz	Plain flour	175 g
	Pinch of salt	
4 oz	Butter	125 g
2	Egg yolks	2
Filling		
½ pint	Milk	300 ml
	Vanilla essence	
4 tbsp	Caster sugar	4×15 ml
2	Medium eggs	2
2 tbsp	Plain flour	2×15 ml
8 oz	Can of pineapple	227 g
	Glacé cherries	
	Angelica	

To make the pastry, sieve icing sugar, flour and salt into a bowl and rub in the softened butter. Add the egg yolks, mix lightly to form a stiff paste and knead quickly to a smooth pastry. Roll into a ball and put in the fridge for 1 hour.

Preheat oven to 375°F (190°C) Gas 5. Roll out pastry thinly and line 15 tartlet tins. Bake blind for 10–12 minutes. Remove from oven, leave to cool, then remove from tins.

To make the confectioner's custard, put the milk and vanilla essence into a saucepan and bring to the boil. Remove from heat.

Cream the sugar and eggs in a bowl then stir in flour and gradually add hot milk. Return mixture to pan and slowly bring back to the boil, stirring constantly, for 1–2 minutes. Remove from heat. Cover with damp greaseproof paper to prevent a skin forming.

When custard is cold, put a spoonful into each pastry case. Top with glazed pineapple. Decorate tartlets with glacé cherries and pieces of angelica.

Crème caramel

Overall timing 1–1¼ hours plus overnight chilling

Freezing Not suitable

To serve 8–10

5 oz	**Caster sugar**	**150 g**
¼ pint	**Cold water**	**150 ml**
5	**Large eggs**	**5**
1¼ pint	**Milk**	**750 ml**
½	**Vanilla pod** *or*	**½**
1	**Piece of lemon rind**	**1**

Preheat the oven to 300°F (150°C) Gas 2.

Put 4 oz (125 g) of the sugar in a small pan with the water and dissolve sugar over a gentle heat. When sugar is dissolved bring to boil and boil, without stirring, until it turns a rich golden brown. Pour at once into a warmed 2 pint (1.2 litre) china or ceramic soufflé dish, or use a deep cake tin, and turn so the caramel coats the base and sides of dish.

Meanwhile, whisk together the eggs and remaining sugar. Heat the milk, with the vanilla pod or lemon rind, in the same pan as used for caramel, until warm (do not boil). Remove vanilla pod or lemon rind and pour on to the whisked eggs, stirring.

Strain into the caramel-lined dish and place in a roasting tin, containing 1 inch (2.5cm) of cold water. Cook in oven for 1–1¼ hours or until custard is set. Remove from water bath and leave to cool.

Chill for several hours, or preferably overnight, before turning out of dish on to a serving plate.

Cakes, gâteaux and cheesecakes

Raisin and rum cake

Overall timing 1 hour

Freezing Suitable

To serve 8–12

4 oz	Butter	100 g
4 oz	Caster sugar	100 g
2	Eggs	2
1	Egg yolk	1
5 oz	Plain flour	150 g
4 oz	Raisins	100 g
3 oz	Chopped candid peel	75 g
	Grated rind of 1 lemon	
2 tbsp	Rum	2×15 ml

Preheat the oven to 450°F (230°C) Gas 8.

Cream the butter and sugar together until light and fluffy. Beat in the eggs and egg yolk, one at a time. Sift in the flour and mix well, then fold in the raisins, peel, lemon rind and rum.

Turn into a lined loaf tin. Bake for 5 minutes, then reduce the heat to 350°F (180°C) Gas 4 and bake for a further 40 minutes.

Turn out on to a wire rack and cool. Serve cut into slices.

Parkin

Overall timing 1½ hours

Freezing Suitable

To serve 16

2 oz	Butter	50 g
2 oz	Lard	50 g
8 oz	Black treacle	225 g
4 oz	Golden syrup	125 g
8 oz	Plain flour	225 g
2 teasp	Baking powder	2×5 ml
2 teasp	Ground ginger	2×5 ml
8 oz	Coarse oatmeal	225 g
4 oz	Dark soft brown sugar	125 g
¼ pint	Milk	150 ml

Preheat the oven to 350°F (180°C) Gas 4.

Put the butter and lard in a small pan and melt over a gentle heat. Add the treacle and syrup and heat till runny. Sift the flour, baking powder and ginger into a large bowl. Stir in the oatmeal and brown sugar. Make a well in the centre. Pour in the fat and treacle mixture and half the milk. Mix to a soft pouring consistency, adding more milk as necessary.

Pour into a greased and bottom-lined 8 inch (20cm) square cake tin. Bake for about 1 hour or until firm to the touch. Leave to cool in the tin.

To serve cut into squares.

Coconut cake

Overall timing 1¾ hours

Freezing Suitable: without topping

Cuts into 12 pieces		
5 oz	**Plain flour**	**150 g**
3 oz	**Margarine**	**75 g**
Filling and Topping		
4 oz	**Margarine**	**125 g**
4 oz	**Caster sugar**	**125 g**
4	**Eggs**	**4**
3 tbsp	**Cocoa**	**3×15 ml**
2 tbsp	**Crème de cacao**	**2×15 ml**
6 oz	**Desiccated coconut**	**175 g**
3fl oz	**Milk**	**90 ml**
2 tbsp	**Plain flour**	**2×15 ml**
½ teasp	**Lemon juice**	**2.5 ml**
3 oz	**Icing sugar**	**75 g**

Put flour in a bowl. Rub in fat, stir in 4 teasp (4×5 ml) cold water till smooth. Chill 30 minutes.

Preheat oven to 425°F (220°C) Gas 7. Grease a 10 inch (25cm) cake tin. Roll dough to fit base. Prick with fork; bake 10 minutes.

Separate 3 eggs. Cream fat, add caster sugar, 1 whole egg, 2 egg yolks, cocoa, liqueur, coconut and milk. Mix well; stir in sifted flour. Spread over base; cook 15 minutes. Cool a little. Reduce oven to 300°F (150°C) Gas 2.

Whip 3 egg whites with lemon juice till soft peaks form. Add icing sugar; beat till stiff. Pour over cake; fork over. Cook 30–35 minutes. Cool on a wire rack.

Aniseed tea-bread

Overall timing 1 hour 10 minutes

Freezing Suitable

To serve 12		
5	**Eggs**	**5**
6 oz	**Caster sugar**	**175 g**
6 oz	**Plain flour**	**175 g**
1 tbsp	**Ground aniseed**	**15 ml**
2 teasp	**Dried yeast**	**2×5 ml**
3 tbsp	**Lukewarm water**	**3×15 ml**

Preheat oven to 425°F (220°C) Gas 7.

Separate eggs. In a bowl whisk together the yolks and 5 oz (150 g) of the sugar till mixture leaves trails. Mix in flour gradually so no lumps are formed, then add aniseed.

Stir the yeast into the lukewarm water and leave to stand for 5 minutes.

Whisk egg whites till very stiff. Stir yeast liquid into creamed mixture, then gently fold in whisked egg whites. Pour into a well-greased and bottom-lined 10 inch (25cm) round cake tin. Bake for about 40 minutes or until firm when pressed in the centre. Turn out of tin on to a wire rack and sprinkle with remaining sugar.

Coconut and cherry surprise

Overall timing 1 hour

Freezing Suitable: reheat in 375°F (190°C) Gas 5 oven for 10 minutes

To serve 8–10		
8 oz	**Shortcrust pastry**	**225 g**
2½ oz	**Ground almonds**	**65 g**
14 oz	**Can of cherry pie filling**	**379 g**
1 oz	**Desiccated coconut**	**25 g**
Filling		
3 oz	**Butter**	**75 g**
3 oz	**Caster sugar**	**75 g**
2	**Eggs**	**2**
¼ teasp	**Almond essence**	**1.25 ml**
2 tbsp	**Milk**	**2×15 ml**
2 oz	**Self-raising flour**	**50 g**
2 oz	**Desiccated coconut**	**50 g**
1½ oz	**Ground almonds**	**40 g**

Topping		
3 tbsp	**Desiccated coconut**	**3×15 ml**
1	**Egg yolk**	**1**
1 teasp	**Milk**	**5 ml**

Roll out dough and use to line greased 10 inch (25cm) springform tin. Sprinkle ground almonds over. Spread pie filling to within 1 inch (2.5cm) of edge, then cover with coconut.

Preheat the oven to 400°F (200°C) Gas 6.

Make filling by creaming butter with sugar till pale and fluffy. Add eggs, essence and 1 tbsp (15 ml) milk and beat well. Fold in flour, followed by remaining milk, coconut and almonds.

Place mixture in blobs over pie filling and smooth evenly so no fruit is visible. Sprinkle with coconut and bake for 30 minutes.

Mix egg yolk and milk together. Brush over tart and bake a further 10 minutes. Serve hot.

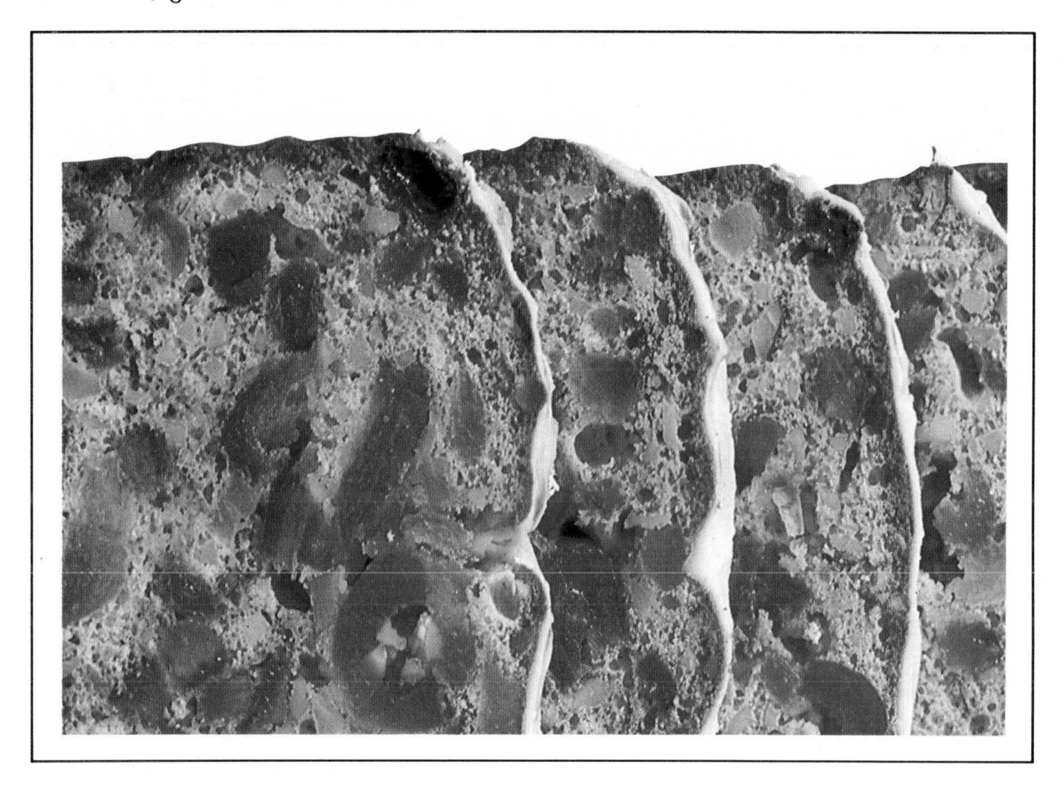

Fruity nut loaf

Overall timing 2 hours plus cooling time

Freezing Not suitable

Cut into 20 slices

4 oz	Brazil nut kernels	125 g
4 oz	Dates	125 g
4 oz	Dried apricots	125 g
4 oz	Sultanas	125 g
2 oz	Candied peel	50 g
2 oz	Glacé cherries	50 g
4	Large eggs	4
5 oz	Granulated sugar	150 g
	Vanilla essence	
4 teasp	Rum	4×5 ml
9 oz	Plain flour	250 g
2 teasp	Baking powder	2×5 ml
3½ oz	Icing sugar	100 g
2 teasp	Hot water	2×5 ml
1 teasp	Lemon juice	5 ml

Preheat oven to 350°F (180°C) Gas 4. Line a 2 lb (900 g) loaf tin with greased greaseproof paper.

Chop nuts. Stone dates and chop. Cut apricots into strips. Mix raisins with candied peel in a bowl. Halve the cherries and add.

Lightly whisk the eggs in another bowl. Mix in the sugar and whisk till pale cream and foamy. Stir in a few drops of vanilla essence and 3 teasp (3×5 ml) rum, then sieve in the flour and baking powder. Beat the mixture till smooth.

Add the fruit and stir well. Spoon mixture into prepared tin and cook in the middle of the oven for about 1–1½ hours till well risen and golden. Remove cake from oven. Cool for 30 minutes in tin. then turn cake on to a wire rack and peel off the paper. Allow to cool.

To make the glacé icing, sieve the icing sugar into a bowl. Quickly mix in the hot water, lemon juice and remaining rum then, pour icing over the cold cake.

All-bran loaf

Overall timing 2½ hours

Freezing Suitable

Makes 1 loaf

2 oz	**All-Bran**	**50 g**
5 oz	**Muscovado sugar**	**150 g**
4 oz	**Chopped dates or dried fruit**	**125 g**
8fl oz	**Milk**	**220 ml**
	Pinch of salt	
1 teasp	**Allspice**	**5 ml**
6 oz	**Plain wholemeal flour**	**175 g**
1½ teasp	**Baking powder**	**7.5 ml**
2 oz	**Vegetable margarine**	**50 g**

In a bowl mix together bran, sugar fruit, milk and salt and leave to soak for 1 hour.

Preheat oven to 375°F (190°C) Gas 5. Sift allspice, flour and baking powder together, then mix into fruit with melted margarine. Beat well. Place in greased 1 lb (450 g) loaf tin. Bake for 1 minute in centre of oven. Turn out on to wire rack to cool. When cold, serve sliced and buttered. Ice, if liked.

Dublin fruit cake

Overall timing 2½ hours

Freezing Not suitable

To serve 10–12

8 oz	Plain flour	225 g
	Salt	
6 oz	Softened butter	175 g
6 oz	Soft brown sugar	175 g
3	Eggs	3
8 oz	Sultanas	225 g
8 oz	Seedless raisins	225 g
2 oz	Mixed chopped candied peel	50 g
2 oz	Glacé cherries	50 g
	Grated rind of 1 lemon	
3 tbsp	Milk or whiskey	3×15 ml

Line bottom and sides of a deep 7–8 inch (18–20cm) round cake tin with greased greaseproof paper. Preheat the oven to 325°F (170°C) Gas 3.

Sift the flour and a pinch of salt into a mixing bowl. Cream the butter and sugar together in another mixing bowl until light and fluffy. Beat in the eggs, one at a time, adding a little of the flour between each egg. Beat in the remaining flour, then stir in the dried and candied fruits, lemon rind and enough milk or whiskey to give a soft but not sticky mixture.

Spoon cake mixture into tin and smooth top with a flat-bladed knife or spatula. Bake in the centre of the oven for about 2 hours or till a skewer inserted in the centre comes out clean. Remove from oven and cool in tin.

Banana and almond loaf

Overall timing 1¼ hours. This cake is better made 1–2 days before it is to be eaten

Freezing Suitable: without icing

Cuts into 8 slices

3½ oz	Butter or margarine	100 g
3½ oz	Caster sugar	100 g
2	Eggs	2
8 oz	Self-raising flour	225 g
½ teasp	Mixed spice	2.5 ml
	Pinch of salt	
4 tbsp	Milk	4×15 ml
3	Bananas	3
1 tbsp	Lemon juice	15 ml
2 oz	Flaked almonds	50 g
	Icing sugar (optional)	

Grease and base-line a 2 lb (900 g) loaf tin. Preheat oven to 375°F (190°C) Gas 5. Cream the butter (or margarine) and sugar in a bowl until pale and fluffy. Beat in the eggs one at a time. Sieve the flour, spice and salt together. Add to egg mixture gradually, beating well in between each addition. Gradually beat in the milk.

Peel the bananas and cut in half lengthways. Sprinkle with lemon juice to prevent discoloration.

Put half the creamed mixture in the prepared tin. Cover with a layer of bananas and half the almonds. Cover with remaining creamed mixture then scatter rest of almonds over the top.

Cook in the centre of the oven for about 55 minutes until well risen and golden brown. Leave to cool in tin, then turn out and peel away lining paper. Before serving, dredge with icing sugar for a pretty finish.

Banana cake

Overall timing 2¼ hours plus cooling. This cake tastes even better if kept for 24 hours

Freezing Suitable

Cuts into 8 slices

2 lb	Bananas	900 g
4	Eggs	4
6 oz	Butter	175 g
12 oz	Granulated sugar	350 g
14 oz	Self-raising flour	400 g
1 teasp	Salt	5 ml
½ teasp	Bicarbonate of soda	2.5 ml
6 oz	Chopped walnuts	175 g
Icing		
12 oz	Icing sugar	350 g
1 tbsp	Cocoa	15 ml
2 oz	Butter	50 g
	Vanilla essence	

Grease and flour an 8 inch (20cm) cake tin. Preheat oven to 350°F (180°C) Gas 4.

Put 1 banana aside for the icing and mash the rest to a smooth purée. Beat the eggs. In a large bowl, cream the butter, adding sugar slowly till pale and fluffy. Beat in the eggs, then the bananas. Beat well till smooth.

Stir in the flour, salt and soda. Add nuts and quickly pour the mixture into prepared tin. Cook in centre of the oven for 1½–2 hours or until a skewer inserted comes out clean. Turn out on to a cake rack and leave to cool.

To make icing, mash reserved banana to a purée. Place butter and cocoa in a pan and heat till butter melts. Pour into banana mixture. Beat well. Add sifted icing sugar and stir to make a good consistency. Add a few drops of vanilla essence. Leave for a few minutes then spread on cake.

Nut bread

Overall timing 1¾ hours plus cooling

Freezing Not suitable

Cuts into 12 slices

16 oz	Plain flour	450 g
4 oz	Caster sugar	125 g
½ teasp	Salt	2.5 ml
3 teasp	Baking powder	3×5 ml
1 tbsp	Cinnamon	15 ml
2 oz	Butter	50 g
4 oz	Chopped mixed nuts	125 g
2	Eggs	2
8fl oz	Milk	220 ml
3 tbsp	Orange juice	3×15 ml

Preheat oven to 350°F (180°C) Gas 4. Sieve flour, sugar, salt, baking powder and cinnamon into a bowl. Cut and fold in butter, then add the nuts.

Beat the eggs till fluffy in a jug, then beat in the milk. Pour into the flour mixture, add orange juice and knead together quickly.

Pour mixture into greased 2 lb (900 g) loaf tin and bake in oven for about 1½ hours. It will be cooked when a skewer comes out clean. Remove from oven.

Leave for 5 minutes then ease out of tin and place on wire rack. Serve sliced and buttered on the day of making – this sort of bread does not store well.

Cream sponge

Overall timing 25–30 minutes plus cooling

Freezing Suitable: without filling and topping

Cuts into 8 slices

4	Large eggs	4
6 oz	Caster sugar	175 g
2 tbsp	Warm water	2×15 ml
4 oz	Plain flour	125 g
1 teasp	Baking powder	5 ml
2 oz	Butter	50 g
2 tbsp	Milk	2×15 ml
4 tbsp	Apricot jam	4×15 ml
2 oz	Split or flaked almonds	50 g
¼ pint	Carton of double cream	150 ml
2 tbsp	Stawberry jam	2×15 ml

Grease and flour 2 8 inch sandwich tins. Preheat oven to 375°F (190°C) Gas 5.

Separate eggs. Place yolks in mixing bowl and beat till light and fluffy, then add sugar with warm water and beat well. Sift flour and baking powder and mix in a little at a time, alternating with milk. Melt butter and add.

Whip whites till stiff. Use a spatula or metal spoon to fold them carefully into egg/flour mixture. Divide mixture between sandwich tins and cook on centre shelf of oven for 15–20 minutes. When cooked, the sponges will pull away from the sides of the tins. Turn out on to wire rack and leave to cool.

When cold, spread top of one sponge with apricot jam. Place second sponge on top. Whip cream and fold in stawberry jam. Spread cream over top of sponge, then sprinkle almonds over.

American bread tart

Overall timing 1 hour 35 minutes

Freezing Suitable

To serve 8

7 oz	Bread	200 g
1 pint	Milk	560 ml
3	Eggs	3
3 tbsp	Caster sugar	3×15 ml
	Pinch of salt	
¼ teasp	Grated nutmeg	1.25 ml
1 teasp	Vanilla essence	2.5 ml
2 tbsp	Sultanas	2×15 ml
4 tbsp	Chopped dates	4×15 ml
3 tbsp	Chopped almonds	3×15 ml
Decoration		
4 oz	Icing sugar	125 g
2 tbsp	Lemon juice	2×15 ml
2 oz	Cooking chocolate	50 g
	Flaked almonds	

Preheat the oven to 400°F (200°C) Gas 4.

Toast bread. Heat milk and crumble toast into pan. Remove from heat. In a bowl, cream together eggs, sugar and salt. Add nutmeg and vanilla essence, then sultanas, dates, almonds, soaked toast and milk. Mix well.

Grease an 8 or 9 inch (20cm or 23cm) springform tin generously, spoon in the mixture and bake for 1 hour, or until firm and golden brown. Remove from oven, turn out on to wire rack.

Mix icing sugar and lemon juice and spread over the cake. (To make chocolate icing, add 1 tbsp (15 ml) cocoa.)

Melt cooking chocolate over boiling water and, using a piping bag with a fine nozzle, make a criss-cross pattern on top of cake. Toast almonds and sprinkle round edges of cake.

Dijon spice loaf

Overall timing 1½ hours

Freezing Suitable

To serve 12

12 oz	Plain flour	350 g
3 teasp	Baking powder	3×5 ml
	Pinch of salt	
1 teasp	Powdered aniseed	5 ml
	Pinch of cinnamon	
4 oz	Butter or margarine	125 g
¼ pint	Milk	150 ml
7 oz	Thick honey	200 g
3 tbsp	Rum	3×15 ml
2 tbsp	Water	2×15 ml
2	Small eggs	2
2 oz	Blanched almonds	50 g

Preheat oven to 350°F (180°C) Gas 4. Grease and bottom-line loaf tin.

Sieve the flour, baking powder, salt, powdered aniseed and cinnamon into a mixing bowl. Add butter or margarine and rub it in lightly until the mixture resembles fine breadcrumbs.

In a saucepan, heat milk to lukewarm. Remove from heat and add honey. Stir until well blended. Mix in the rum and water. Add to the flour mixture with beaten eggs and beat well.

Pour mixture into prepared tin and arrange almonds on the top. Bake in oven for 1¼ hours.

Remove loaf from oven, turn out of tin on to a wire rack to cool.

Sand cake

Overall timing 1¼ hours

Freezing Suitable: thaw at room temperature for 2 hours

To serve 12

8 oz	Softened butter	225 g
8 oz	Caster sugar	225 g
5	Eggs	5
	Grated rind of 1 lemon	
	Pinch of salt	
5 oz	Potato flour	150 g
3 oz	Plain flour	75 g
	Icing sugar	

Grease and base-line cake tin. Preheat the oven to 375°F (190°C) Gas 5.

Put the butter and sugar in a bowl and whisk till pale and creamy. Separate the eggs. Add the yolks, lemon rind and salt to the bowl and whisk in. Add sifted flours a little at a time, whisking to a smooth, creamy mixture.

In another bowl, whisk egg whites till stiff but not dry, then carefully fold into creamed mixture.

Turn mixture into prepared tin and bake in the oven for about 45 minutes. Cool in tin, then turn out and dredge top with icing sugar. If you prefer, you can cut the finished sponge in half and fill with jam and whipped cream.

Gâteau de patates douces

Overall timing 1½ hours plus chilling

Freezing Not suitable

To serve 6–8

2 lb	**Sweet potatoes**	**900 g**
1 pint	**Milk**	**560 ml**
1	**Vanilla pod**	**1**
5 oz	**Candied fruit**	**150 g**
3 oz	**Butter**	**75 g**
4 oz	**Caster sugar**	**125 g**
2	**Eggs**	**2**
2 tbsp	**Icing sugar**	**2×15 ml**
	Chocolate sauce or pouring cream	

Preheat the oven to 400°F (200°C) Gas 6. Grease and base-line a 6½ inch (16cm) round deep cake tin.

Wash and peel the sweet potatoes and cut into chunks. Put into a large saucepan with the milk and vanilla pod. Bring to the boil and cook over a low heat for about 10 minutes till tender.

Drain, reserving the milk, and remove the vanilla pod. Mash with enough of the milk to give a stiff, smooth consistency.

Chop 4 oz (125 g) of the candied fruit, add to the potato purée with the butter and sugar and mix well. Add the eggs one at a time, beating well between each addition.

Spoon the mixture into the tin, smooth the surface and bake in the centre of the oven for about 1 hour till a skewer inserted in the centre comes out clean.

Allow the cake to cool in the tin, then chill for 2–3 hours before turning out on to a serving plate. Dredge the icing sugar in a ring on top of the cake and decorate with the remaining candied fruit. Serve with hot or cold chocolate sauce or pouring cream.

Dobos cake

Overall timing 1¼ hours

Freezing Suitable without caramel

To serve 8

4	Eggs	4
4 oz	Caster sugar	125 g
4 oz	Plain flour	125 g
1	Sachet vanilla sugar	1
3 tbsp	Lemon juice	3×15 ml
½ teasp	Grated lemon rind	2.5 ml
½ teasp	Water	2.5 ml
1 oz	Butter	25 g
Chocolate cream		
5 oz	Softened butter	150 g
7 oz	Icing sugar	200 g
3	Egg yolks	3
4 oz	Dark chocolate	125 g
4 tbsp	Water	4×15 ml
Caramel		
3 oz	Caster sugar	75 g
3 tbsp	Water	3×15 ml

Preheat oven to 375°F (190°C) Gas 5. Grease 2 baking trays and 4×8 inch (20cm) cake rings.

Separate eggs. Whisk whites and sift in flour and vanilla sugar; fold in gently. Fold in half the lemon juice, lemon rind and water. Pour a quarter of mixture into each ring on baking trays. Spread out to edges.

Cook near top of oven for 7–10 minutes, until pale golden but still soft. Gently lift on to a wire rack to keep flat and cool.

Make chocolate cream: beat together butter, icing sugar and egg yolks. In a bowl over hot water, melt chocolate with water; beat into butter cream. Spread chocolate cream on 3 cakes; stack on top of each other. Place last sponge on top.

Stir sugar and water in pan until sugar melts. Heat until golden. Stir in remaining lemon juice: pour over cake, spreading evenly with a knife brushed with oil. Mark into 8; leave to set.

Bûche de Noël (Christmas Log)

Overall timing 1 hour plus chilling

Freezing Not suitable

To serve 4–5

Cake		
5	Eggs	5
3 oz	Caster sugar	75 g
4 oz	Plain flour	125 g
¼ oz	Vanilla sugar	10 g
Mocha cream		
8 oz	Softened butter	225 g
4½ oz	Icing sugar	140 g
2 tbsp	Cocoa powder	2×15 ml
2 tbsp	Diluted instant coffee	2×15 ml
½ pint	Carton of double cream	300 ml

Preheat the oven to 350°F (180°C) Gas 4.

Line a large baking tray with buttered wax paper. Separate the eggs. Beat the egg yolks with the sugar until the mixture is very light and fluffy. Stir in the flour and vanilla sugar, a little at a time, then gently fold in the stiffly beaten egg whites.

Spread the mixture evenly on to the wax paper to form a 9×13 inch (23×33 cm) rectangle and bake for 12–15 minutes or until risen and golden.

Transfer immediately on to a dampened tea towel, dusted with sugar and cut off and discard the dry edges of cake. Roll the cake up in the cloth and leave to cool.

To make mocha cream, beat the butter with 2½ oz (65 g) of the icing sugar until light and fluffy and stir in the cocoa and coffee.

Unroll the cake, cover with a thin layer of mocha cream. Whip the cream with the remaining 2 oz (50 g) icing sugar until stiff and spread over cake. Roll up cake again, this time without the cloth.

Cut off the two ends diagonally and cover the cake and these two pieces with the remaining mocha cream. Place the slices on the cake to look like branches of a tree and with a fork, mark lines into cream for bark.

Chill the cake for several hours.

Rice cake

Overall timing 1 hour 10 minutes

Freezing Not suitable

To serve 6–8

4 oz	Blanched almonds	125 g
½ pint	Water	300 ml
1½ pint	Milk	850 ml
6 oz	Caster sugar	175 g
1	Strip of lemon peel	1
6 oz	Ground rice	175 g
4	Eggs	4
10	Small macaroons or ratafias	10
2 oz	Candied peel	50 g
	Butter	
	Fine white breadcrumbs	
	Raspberry sauce (optional)	

Preheat the oven to 350°F (180°C) Gas 4.

Chop the almonds. Place the water, milk, 1 tbsp (15 ml) of the sugar and lemon peel in a pan and bring to the boil. Add ground rice and cook till it has absorbed all the liquid.

Remove pan from heat, discard lemon peel and allow mixture to cool. Separate the eggs. Beat the egg yolks with the remaining sugar, add the chopped almonds, crushed macaroons or ratafias (reserving a few for decorating) and chopped candied peel. Stir in the cooled rice mixture.

Stiffly whisk the egg whites and fold into the mixture lightly, using a metal spoon. Pour the mixture into a 12 inch (30cm) loose-bottomed cake tin, which has been lightly buttered and sprinkled with breadcrumbs.

Bake for 40–45 minutes until cooked through. Turn cake out on to a wire rack and decorate with the reserved macaroons or ratafias. Serve hot or cold with raspberry sauce, if liked.

Chocolate layer cake

Overall timing 57–58 minutes plus cooling

Freezing Suitable: without icing

3	Eggs	3
6 oz	Caster sugar	175 g
3 oz	Butter or margarine	75 g
5½ oz	Plain flour	165 g
5 tbsp	Cocoa powder	5×15 ml
½ oz	Baking powder	15 g
¼ oz	Vanilla sugar	10 g
4fl oz	Milk	120 ml
	Pinch of salt	
Icing		
2	Egg whites	2
11 oz	Caster sugar	300 g
¼ oz	Vanilla sugar	10 g
6 tbsp	Water	6×15 ml

Preheat the oven to 350°F (180°C) Gas 4.

Separate eggs. In a bowl beat together the egg yolks and sugar then add the melted butter or margarine, sifted flour, cocoa and baking powder. Stir in the vanilla sugar, milk and salt then gently fold in the stiffly beaten egg whites.

Pour mixture into a deep 8 inch (20cm) cake tin which has been buttered and dusted with flour. Bake for 45 minutes or until a skewer inserted in the centre comes out clean. Remove from oven, leave to cool and carefully slice into 3 layers.

Make the icing, put the egg whites, caster sugar, vanilla sugar and water in the top of a double boiler and beat the mixture with an electric or rotary whisk for 7–8 minutes or until stiff.

Working quickly, divide mixture between the 3 layers of cake and sandwich cake together. Peak the top layer of icing with a fork and leave the cake to stand for 2–3 hours before serving.

Iced chestnut cake

Overall timing 1 hour 15 minutes plus chilling

Freezing Suitable

To serve 8–10

2 lb	Chestnuts	900 g
1½ pint	Milk	850 ml
3 oz	Caster sugar	75 g
¼	Vanilla pod	¼
	Pinch of salt	
3 oz	Butter or margarine	75 g
2 tbsp	Cocoa powder	2×15 ml
3 oz	Macaroons	75 g
	Rum	
2 oz	Toasted blanched almonds	50 g
¼ pint	Carton of double cream	150 ml
	Marron glacé (optional)	

Peel the chestnuts, soak in boiling water for 5 minutes and remove the skins with a sharp knife.

Bring the milk, sugar, vanilla pod and salt to the boil in a pan then remove the vanilla pod and add the chestnuts. Cook the mixture over low heat for about 1 hour.

Sieve mixture and return to the pan. Cook over a moderate heat, stirring constantly, until it thickens then remove from heat and leave to cool. Stir in the softened butter or margarine, cocoa and rum to taste. Beat the mixture until well blended.

Line a 9 inch (23 cm) high-sided tin or charlotte mould with dampened cheesecloth. Pour in one third of the mixture, add a layer of macaroons soaked in rum, cover with another third of the chestnut mixture, then another layer of macaroons, soaked in rum, and finally the remaining chestnut mixture.

Place in fridge for a few hours or overnight, then turn out on to a serving dish and remove the cheesecloth. Press the chopped toasted almonds around side of cake and decorate with whipped cream and marron glacé if liked.

Meringue cuite

Overall timing 55 minutes – 1 hour 10 minutes

Freezing Suitable

2	**Medium or large egg whites**	2
4½ oz	**Icing sugar**	140 g

Preheat the oven to 300°F (150°C) Gas 2.

Put the egg whites and icing sugar in a bowl standing over a saucepan containing 1 inch (2.5cm) hot water.

Whisk ingredients together well till thick enough to stand in stiff peaks. Turn off the heat when the water reaches simmering point.

Use mixture for making shells or meringue baskets, or piping rosettes. Bake on the lowest shelf of the oven for 45 minutes – 1 hour till crisp and dry. Store in an airtight tin.

Variation

Meringue cuite can also be used for topping desserts. Dredge caster sugar over to give a crisp top and soft inside and cook at 400°F (200°C) Gas 6 for about 20 minutes till golden. The meringue will not dry out if used in this way.

Elisa's spicy confection

Overall timing 1 hour plus cooling

Freezing Not suitable

Cuts into 32

	Rice paper	
12 oz	**Unblanches almonds**	**350 g**
1 lb	**Granulated sugar**	**450 g**
½ pint	**Milk**	**300 ml**
2 oz	**Butter**	**50 g**
½ teasp	**Ground aniseed**	**2.5 ml**
½ teasp	**Ground cinnamon**	**2.5 ml**
½ teasp	**Ground cardamom**	**2.5 ml**
2 oz	**Plain dessert chocolate**	**50 g**
8 oz	**Caster sugar**	**225 g**
5 tbsp	**Water**	**5×15 ml**
	Cream of tartar	
1	**Egg white**	**1**
2 teasp	**Lemon juice**	**2×5 ml**

Grease and base-line an 8 inch (20 cm) round cake tin using rice paper. Spread almonds on baking tray and cook under a moderate grill for 10 minutes, turning frequently, till crisp and dry. Cool.

Put granulated sugar, milk, butter and spices into pan and stir over a low heat till sugar dissolves.

Boil steadily without stirring to 240°F (116°C). Grate chocolate.

Remove from heat and place on a cold surface to prevent further cooking. Add chocolate and beat till thick. Quickly stir in almonds and pour into tin. Smooth top; leave to cool. When cold remove from tin and place on a wire rack over a plate. Put caster sugar, water and a pinch of cream of tartar into a pan; heat gently, stirring, till sugar dissolves.

Bring to the boil without stirring and boil to 240°F (116°C). Remove from heat. Whisk egg white till stiff but not dry. Pour syrup in a thin stream into egg white, whisking constantly. Quickly add lemon juice, mix well and pour over cake. Spread over top and sides and leave to set.

Rum and raisin cheesecake

Overall timing 1 hour 55 minutes plus chilling and cooling

Freezing Suitable

To serve 10–12

Base		
4 oz	Plain flour	125 g
2	Egg yolks	2
2 oz	Caster sugar	50 g
¼ teasp	Vanilla essence	1.25 ml
	Pinch of salt	
2 oz	Softened butter	50 g
Filling		
3 oz	Large stoned raisins	75 g
4 fl oz	Rum	120 ml
1 lb	Curd cheese	450 g
4 oz	Softened butter	125 g
4 oz	Caster sugar	125 g
	Grated rind of 1 lemon	
4	Eggs	4

Preheat the oven to 400°F (200°C) Gas 6. To make cheesecake base, put flour on to a work surface. Make a well in centre and add the egg yolks, sugar, vanilla and salt. Add the butter in pieces and quickly knead mixture together to make a dough. Wrap and chill for 30 minutes.

Roll out dough and use to line the base and sides of an 8 inch (20 cm) springform or loose-bottomed cake tin. Prick with a fork then bake blind in centre of the oven for 20 minutes.

Meanwhile wash raisins and place in pan with the rum. Bring to boiling point, remove from heat, cover and leave.

Push curd cheese through a sieve into bowl. Add softened butter, sugar and lemon rind and beat till well combined. Add eggs and beat till creamy, then stir in cooled raisin and rum mixture.

Remove base from oven. Reduce temperature to 350°F (180°C) Gas 4. Pour cheese mixture into tin, smooth top and bake in the centre of oven for 1 hour 10 minutes. Cool in tin. Run lightly oiled knife round edges before releasing the spring. Serve chilled.

Granny's cheesecake

Overall timing 1 hour plus cooling and chilling

Freezing Suitable

To serve 10–12

8 oz	Plain chocolate digestive biscuits	225 g
4 oz	Butter	125 g
8 oz	Cream cheese	225 g
8 oz	Curd cheese	225 g
2	Eggs	2
6 oz	Caster sugar	175 g
1 teasp	Vanilla essence	5 ml
½ pint	Carton of soured cream	284 ml
1	Lemon	1

Preheat the oven to 375°F (190°C) Gas 5. Grease and base-line an 8 inch springform or loose-bottomed cake tin.

Crush biscuits with a rolling pin. Reserve 2 tbsp (2×15 ml) of the crumbs. Melt butter in a saucepan, remove from heat and stir in the crumbs. Spread crumb mixture evenly over tin base.

Place both cheeses in a large bowl and beat until well blended. Place the eggs and 4 oz (125 g) of the sugar in a bowl and whisk until beaters leave a trail. Add essence.

Gradually add the egg mixture to the cheeses, whisking all the time to give a smooth, creamy conistency. Pour on to the crumb base and bake in the centre of the oven for 35–40 mintues until firm (gently shake tin: if centre doesn't wobble, cake is cooked).

Grate the rind of the lemon, then squeeze the juice. Place rind in bowl with soured cream and remaining sugar. Beat well. Add 2 tbsp (30 ml) of the lemon juice and mix well. Pour the mixture over the top of the cooked cake, return it to the oven for a further 10 minutes.

Remove from oven and sprinkle with remaining crumbs. Allow to cool, then chill, preferably overnight.

Storecupboard cheesecake

Overall timing 25 minutes plus chilling and setting

Freezing Suitable: freeze the filling in tin without Crispie base. Make Crispie base and spread over thawed cheesecake. When set, invert on to serving plate. Decorate and chill

To serve 6–8

2 oz	Plain chocolate	50 g
1 oz	Rice Crispies	25 g
1	Tangerine jelly tablet	1
8 oz	Cream cheese	225 g
2	Egg whites	2
11 oz	Can of mandarin oranges	312 g

Break the chocolate into bowl over pan of simmering water and stir gently till melted. Do not overheat or allow water to get into chocolate. When melted, remove bowl and stir in Crispies so they are evenly coated.

Line base of an 8 inch (20cm) springform or loose-bottomed cake tin with greaseproof. Cover gently and smoothly with the chocolate mixture. Chill. Break up jelly tablet and place in saucepan. Drain syrup from mardarin oranges and make up to ¼ pint (150 ml) with water. Add 2 tbsp (2×15 ml) of the syrup to jelly, and cook over a very low heat till jelly melts – be careful not to let it boil. Remove from heat and add rest of syrup. Chill until just beginning to set.

Beat cream cheese in bowl till smooth, then gradually beat in syrupy jelly. In a bowl, whisk whites to soft peak stage, then fold gently into cheese and jelly mix. Pour on to crumb base and chill for 3 hours until set. Arrange drained mandarin oranges on top and chill again before serving.

Florentine cheesecake

Overall timing 25 minutes plus cooling and chilling

Freezing Suitable

To serve 8–10

1	8 inch (20cm) sponge cake	1
4 teasp	Gelatine	4×5 ml
2	Eggs	2
4 oz	Caster sugar	125 g
1 lb	Curd cheese	450 g
2	Lemons	2
¼ pint	Carton of double cream	150 ml
1 tbsp	Icing sugar	15 ml

Split sponge in 2 layers. Mix the gelatine with 3 tbsp (3×15 ml) water in a small bowl. When firm, place bowl over simmering water, stir till gelatine dissolves. Separate eggs.

Add the yolks and caster sugar to the bowl and stir over the heat until the mixture coats the back of a spoon. Remove from heat, cool slightly.

Beat cheese in mixing bowl with grated rind and juice of 2 lemons till smooth, then fold in gelatine mixture.

Whisk cream until it just begins to thicken, then fold into the cheese. Whisk the egg whites to soft peaks and fold in gently till even and smooth.

Put the bottom half of the sponge into an 8 inch (20cm) springform or loose-bottomed cake tin. Pour cheese mixture over and cover with other layer of sponge. Chill, preferably overnight. Dredge with icing sugar.

New Zealand cheesecake

Overall timing 1 hour plus cooling and overnight chilling

Freezing Suitable: without topping

Cuts into 8–10

Base		
8½ oz	Digestive biscuits	250 g
4 oz	Butter	125 g
Filling		
1 tbsp	Powdered gelatine	15 ml
4 tbsp	Cold water	4×15 ml
4 oz	Cottage cheese	125 g
5 oz	Natural yoghurt	141 g
2	Large eggs	2
4 oz	Caster sugar	125 g
2 teasp	Grated lemon rind	2×5 ml
2 teasp	Lemon juice	2×5 ml
¼ pint	Double cream	150 ml
Topping		
1 teasp	Arrowroot	5 ml
2 teasp	Orange juice	2×15 ml
3	Kiwifruit	3
1	Large banana	1

Crush biscuits in a blender. Place in bowl. Melt butter; pour into crumbs; mix well.

Press into 8½ inch (21cm) springform greased tin to cover base and sides. Chill 1 hour.

Sprinkle gelatine over cold water; sieve cottage cheese; mix with yoghurt.

Separate eggs. Beat yolks, half the sugar, lemon rind and juice in a bowl till thick. Place bowl over a pan of simmering water; cook 5 minutes, stirring. Add gelatine; stir till dissolved. Remove bowl from heat; cool.

Whip cream till thick and fold into mixture. Stiffly beat egg whites, fold in remaining sugar; fold into egg and cream mixture. Pour on to base; leave to set.

Mix arrowroot and juice in pan. Bring to boil and, when mixture clears, cool.

Peel and slice fruits. Arrange on cheesecake; spoon over glaze. Chill overnight.

Roulade à la crème de menthe

Overall timing 45 minutes plus overnight standing time

Freezing Suitable: without decoration

To serve 6–8

4 oz	Plain dessert chocolate	125 g
4	Large eggs	4
6 oz	Caster sugar	175 g
½ pint	Carton of double cream	284ml
4 tbsp	Crème de menthe	4×15 ml
1 oz	Chocolate squares	25 g

Preheat oven to 350°F (180°C) Gas 4.

Make a case from a 12 inch (30 cm) square of non-stick paper, cutting 1½ inches (4 cm) diagonally through each corner. Fold up the edges to make a "case" 1 inch (2.5 cm) deep and fasten the corners with staples or paper clips. Place case on a greased baking tray.

Break up the chocolate and place in a small bowl over a pan of hot water. Stir till melted, then cool.

Separate eggs. Place yolks in a large bowl, add 4 oz (125 g) caster sugar. Place bowl over a pan of simmering water and whisk till mixture is thick and leaves a trail on surface for 20 seconds. Stir in the cooled chocolate.

In a large bowl, whisk the egg whites until they form soft peaks, then fold gently into the chocolate mixture. Pour the mixture into the paper case, spreading it into the corners. Smooth the surface. Bake just above centre of oven for about 15 minutes or until firm.

Remove from the oven and cover with a damp tea-towel. Leave overnight.

Remove cloth and undo paper case. Crush remaining sugar and spread on greaseproof paper. Invert the roulade on to paper. Trim off the crisp edges.

Whip the cream till soft peaks form and fold in the crème de menthe. Spread two-thirds of the cream over the roulade and roll up. Place on the serving dish. Pipe the remaining cream on top and decorate with halved chocolate squares. Chill before serving.

Caramel ring cake

Overall timing 1¼ hours

Freezing Suitable: ice cake after thawing

To serve 12		
4 oz	**Butter**	**125 g**
6 oz	**Soft brown sugar**	**175 g**
1 tbsp	**Golden syrup**	**15 ml**
2	**Eggs**	**2**
6 oz	**Self-raising flour**	**175 g**
1 teasp	**Ground cinnamon**	**5 ml**
	Pinch of salt	
¼ teasp	**Bicarbonate of soda**	**1.25 ml**
3fl oz	**Milk**	**90 ml**
	Vanilla essence	

Icing		
1 oz	**Butter**	**25 g**
2 tbsp	**Golden syrup**	**2×15 ml**
1 tbsp	**Milk**	**15 ml**
1 teasp	**Vanilla essence**	**5 ml**
8 oz	**Icing sugar**	**225 g**
1 tbsp	**Ground cinnamon**	**15 ml**

Preheat oven to 350°F (180°C) Gas 4.

Cream butter with sugar; beat in eggs and syrup. Sift in flour, cinnamon and salt and beat well. Mix soda with milk and a few drops of vanilla essence and add to mixture. Place in a greased and floured 9½ inch (24cm) ring tin and bake for 45–50 minutes. Cool on wire rack.

For the icing, heat butter and golden syrup in saucepan. Stir in milk and essence and remove from heat. Sift half of icing sugar and the cinnamon into saucepan and stir well. Stir in rest of sifted sugar.

Pour icing over cake and smooth with spatula dipped in hot water.

Double-iced cherry ring cake

Overall timing 1 ¾ hours

Freezing Suitable: without decoration

To serve 12		
7 oz	Butter	200 g
7 oz	Sugar	200 g
3	Eggs	3
1 teasp	Vanilla essence	5 ml
	Pinch of salt	
1 lb	Plain flour	450 g
2 teasp	Baking powder	2×5 ml
5 tbsp	Milk	5×15 ml
4 tbsp	Rum	4×15 ml
9 oz	Canned cherries	250 g
9 oz	Icing sugar	250 g

Decoration		
12	Fresh cherries	12
1 oz	Caster sugar	25 g

Preheat the oven to 350°F (180°C) Gas 4.

Cream together butter and sugar in a mixing bowl. Separate the eggs. Add yolks to creamed mixture with the vanilla essence and salt. Mix in the flour and baking powder, then milk and 2 tbsp (2×15 ml) rum alternately. Beat 2 egg whites till stiff; fold into mixture.

Drain cherries, saving 4 tbsp (4×15 ml) of juice. Add cherries to mixture, then pour into greased 9½ inch (24cm) ring tin. Bake for 1–1¼ hours. Remove from tin and cool on a wire rack.

To make the icing, mix 5 oz (150 g) of the icing sugar with reserved cherry juice and pour over the top of the cake, leaving it to drip down the sides. Mix remaining rum and 1 tbsp (15 ml) water with rest of icing sugar and pour over the first icing.

Wash and dry cherries. Dip first into remaining egg white, then caster sugar. Arrange on top of cake and leave to set.

Chocolate torte

Overall timing 2 hours

Freezing Suitable (cake only)

To serve 12

8	Eggs	8
8 oz	Caster sugar	225 g
7 oz	Self-raising flour	200 g
4 oz	Ground almonds	125 g
5 oz	Plain chocolate	150 g
2 tbsp	Cocoa	2×15 ml
4 oz	Melted butter	125 g
2 oz	Chocolate flake	50 g
Chocolate cream		
8 oz	Milk cooking chocolate	225 g
1 teasp	Instant coffee	5 ml
2 tbsp	Caster sugar	2×15 ml
1¼ pints	Single cream	700 ml
4 teasp	Powdered gelatine	4×5 ml

Preheat oven to 350°F (180°C) Gas 4. Separate eggs. Beat yolks and 6 oz (175 g) of the sugar till light and fluffy. In another bowl, beat remaining sugar and egg whites till very stiff. Gently fold whites into yolk mixture. Mix flour, almonds, grated chocolate and cocoa in a bowl. Fold into egg mixture followed by butter.

Divide between 2 greased and base-lined 9 inch (23cm) cake tins. Bake for 50 minutes. Cool for 20 minutes in tins, then turn out on to a wire rack.

Meanwhile, place chocolate in a bowl over a pan of boiling water. Add coffee, sugar and cream and stir until chocolate has melted. Remove pan from heat.

Dissolve gelatine in 1 tbsp (15 ml) of water. Add to chocolate mixture, mix well, then pour into a large mixing bowl. Leave to cool, then beat till very stiff.

When cakes are cold, cut each into 2 layers. Sandwich together with chocolate cream and also cover top and sides. Decorate sides with crushed chocolate flake.

Tropical corn cake

Overall timing 1¼ hours

Freezing Suitable: decorate after thawing

To serve 4		
4 oz	Soft vegetable margarine	125 g
1¾ pints	Milk	1 litre
4 oz	Muscovado sugar	125 g
½ teasp	Vanilla essence	2.5 ml
8 oz	Fine cornmeal	225 g
3	Eggs	3
	Salt	
Decoration		
	Fresh pineapple	
9	Glacé cherries	9

Preheat the oven to 350°F (180°C) Gas 4. Use 1 oz (25 g) of the margarine to grease 9 inch (23cm) cake tin.

Put milk, sugar and vanilla in a saucepan and bring to the boil. Stir cornmeal into milk lavishly, to prevent lumps forming. Remove pan from heat.

Separate eggs. Add egg yolks to pan, one at a time, beating well after each addition. Just melt remaining margarine and beat in.

In a bowl, beat the egg whites with a pinch of salt till soft peaks form. Carefully fold whites into cake mixture with a metal spoon. Pour mixture into tin and bake in centre of oven for about 40 minutes.

Turn cake on to wire rack to cool. Place on plate and decorate with fresh pineapple and glacé cherries.

Creamy choux cake

Overall timing 1¾ hours

Freezing Not suitable

To serve 12

4 oz	Plain flour	125 g
8fl oz	Water	220 ml
3 oz	Unsalted butter	75 g
¼ teasp	Salt	1.25 ml
3	Eggs	3
Filling		
8 oz	Curd cheese	225 g
¼ pint	Milk	150 ml
4 tbsp	Caster sugar	4×15 ml
½ pint	Carton of whipping cream	284 ml
½ teasp	Vanilla essence	2.5 ml
15 oz	Can of fruit cocktail	425 g
4	Sponge fingers	4
	Icing sugar	

Preheat the oven to 425°F (220°C) Gas 7. Line two baking trays with greaseproof paper and draw an 8 inch (20cm) circle on each.

Sift flour. Put water, butter and salt into saucepan and bring to the boil, stirring to melt butter. Remove from heat and beat in flour all at once. Return to heat and beat till dough pulls away from sides of pan. Gradually beat in eggs to make a soft, glossy dough.

Divide choux paste and spread evenly inside circles almost to the edge. Bake for 45 minutes. Cool.

Put curd cheese, milk and sugar in a bowl and beat well. Whip cream and vanilla essence in another bowl till soft peaks form, then fold into curd cheese mixture. Reserve one-third of the cream mixture. Drain canned fruit and mix into remaining cream mixture.

Sandwich choux rounds together with cream and fruit mixture. Spread reserved cream over top and cover with crumbled sponge fingers. Dredge with icing sugar.

Richmond maids of honour

Overall timing 1 hour plus overnight draining

Freezing Not suitable

Makes 20

1 pint	Milk	560 ml
1 teasp	Rennet essence *or*	5 ml
1	Junket tablet	1
7½ oz	Packet of frozen puff pastry	212 g
3 oz	Unsalted butter	75 g
2 tbsp	Caster sugar	2×15 ml
2 oz	Nibbed almonds	50 g
1 tbsp	Brandy	15 ml
2	Eggs	2

Put the milk into a saucepan and warm gently to blood heat. Remove from the heat and stir in the rennet or crush and add the junket tablet. Stir for 1 minute, then leave in a warm place for 15–20 minutes or until set.

Put the junket into a piece of muslin, hang it up over a bowl and leave to drain overnight to make curds.

The next day, thaw pastry and preheat the oven to 425°F (220°C) Gas 7.

Roll out the pastry on a floured surface and cut out 20 circles with the pastry cutter. Use to line the bun trays. Place the butter in a bowl and whisk with the sugar, almonds and brandy. Whisk in the eggs to give a frothy mixture. Carefully stir in the drained curds, and divide the mixture between the pastry cases, half-filling them.

Bake in the centre of the oven for 15–20 minutes till well risen and golden. Serve warm or cold.

Treacle and nut slices

Overall timing 2 hours

Freezing Not suitable

Makes 24

5 oz	Plain wholemeal flour	150 g
10 oz	Demerara sugar	275 g
5 tbsp	Vegetable oil	5×15 ml
12 oz	Chopped nuts	350 g
6 oz	Fresh wholemeal breadcrumbs	175 g
	Grated rind of 1 orange	
1	Large cooking apple	1
2	Eggs	2
6 oz	Treacle	175 g

Sift flour into a bowl, add 2 oz (50 g) sugar and oil and mix to make a soft dough. Chill.

Meanwhile, mix nuts with remaining sugar, breadcrumbs and orange rind. Peel and quarter the apple and grate into mixture. Add eggs and treacle and mix well.

Preheat the oven to 350°F (180°C) Gas 4. Divide the dough into 3 equal portions. Roll out each piece thinly to a rectangle the same size as 12×9 inch (30×23cm) baking tin. Place 1 rectangle in bottom of tin, spread half filling over and smooth top. Cover with another piece of dough, spread remaining filling over and add remaining dough.

Bake in the centre of the oven for 1 hour till a skewer inserted in centre comes out clean. Cool, then cut lengthways into 4 strips and diagonally across the strips.

Peach and jam cake

Overall timing 15 minutes plus maceration

Freezing Not suitable

To serve 8

29 oz	Can of peach halves	823 g
5 tbsp	Rum, Kirsch or brandy	5×15 ml
1	8 inch (20cm) sponge cake	1
6 tbsp	Raspberry jam	6×15 ml
¼ pint	Carton of double cream	150 ml
1 oz	Toasted flaked almonds	25 g

Drain peaches and reserve ½ pint (300 ml) of the syrup. Add alcohol to reserved syrup and pour over peaches. Leave for 1 hour to macerate.

Cut sponge cake in two layers. Place bottom layer on serving dish. Drain peaches, spooning half the macerating syrup over the cake till it is moist but still firm. Spread jam over cake, top with second cake layer and spoon remaining syrup over.

Beat cream in a bowl till thick enough to pipe. Spread a thin layer over the top and sides of the cake. Spoon the rest of the cream into a piping bag. Arrange the peach halves on top of the cake, cut side down, and pipe swirls of cream between them. Press the flaked almonds on to the sides of the cake. Chill before serving.

Fruit tartlets

Overall timing 15 minutes plus pastry and crème pâtissière preparation times

Freezing Not suitable

Pastry		
12 oz	**Plain flour**	350 g
6 oz	**Butter or margarine**	175 g
3 oz	**Caster sugar**	75 g
2	**Egg yolks**	2
1 tbsp	**Marsala**	15 ml
1	**Lemon**	1
	Pinch of salt	
1	**Quantity of Crème Pâtissière (recipe page 32, Tarte aux poires)**	1
Fruit filling and Glaze		
	Sliced banana	
	Canned cherries	
	Black or green grapes	
	Canned pineapple pieces	
8 oz	**Apricot jam**	225 g
2 tbsp	**Water or rum**	2×15 ml

Preheat the oven to 400°F (200°C) Gas 6.

To make the pastry, sift the flour on to a board and make a well in centre. Add the butter or margarine, sugar, egg yolks, Marsala, finely grated rind of lemon and salt. Work the ingredients together quickly to form a dough then shape into a ball, wrap and chill for 30 minutes.

Meanwhile make crème pâtissière, see page 32, Tarte aux poires.

Roll out pastry thinly, cut into 4 inch (10cm) circles and use to line small tartlet moulds. Add a circle of foil to each one and fill with baking beans. Bake for 15 minutes. Remove foil and beans and leave to cool.

Put 1 tbsp (15 ml) of the cooled crème pâtissière in each tartlet case and top with sliced banana, cherries, grapes and pineapple.

Heat the jam until melted then sieve and stir in the water or rum. Brush glaze over fruit while still warm. Leave to set before serving.

Eccles cakes

Overall timing 30 minutes

Freezing Suitable

Makes 12

9 oz	Puff pastry	250 g
6 oz	Currants	175 g
2 oz	Candied peel	50 g
1 oz	Demerara sugar	25 g
1 oz	Butter	25 g
½ teasp	Ground mixed spice	2.5 ml
1	Egg white	1
	Caster sugar	

Preheat oven to 425°F (220°C) Gas 7.

Roll out pastry on a lightly floured board to a large rectangle and cut out twelve 4 inch (10cm) rounds.

Mix together currants, peel, sugar, butter and spice. Place a little of the mixture in the centre of each pastry round. Moisten pastry edges, pull together into centre to cover filling and seal firmly. Place, join side down, on dampened baking trays. Flatten slightly, then make 2 or 3 cuts on top with a sharp knife.

Brush with lightly beaten egg white and dredge with caster sugar. Bake for 10–12 minutes till well risen and golden. Serve warm or cold.

Treacle raisin sponge

Overall timing 1¾ hours

Freezing Suitable: without icing sugar topping

To serve 12

4 oz	Butter	125 g
6 oz	Treacle	175 g
2 oz	Golden syrup	50 g
8 oz	Plain flour	225 g
1 teasp	Mixed spice	5 ml
2 oz	Caster sugar	50 g
1 teasp	Bicarbonate of soda	5 ml
	Grated rind of 1 lemon	
2	Eggs	2
¼ pint	Milk	150 ml
4 oz	Raisins	125 g
2 tbsp	Icing sugar	2×15 ml

Preheat the oven to 325°F (170°C) Gas 3.

Put the butter, treacle and syrup into a saucepan and heat gently till butter melts. Remove from the heat and allow to cool slightly. Sift the flour, spice, sugar and soda into a large bowl and make a well in the centre. Add the lemon rind, eggs and treacle mixture and beat well, adding the milk gradually, till smooth. Stir in the raisins.

Pour into a greased and bottom-lined 8½ inch (22cm) round cake tin. Bake for 1¼–1½ hours till springy when pressed lightly. Leave to cool in the tin for 5 minutes, then turn out to cool completely. Dust liberally with icing sugar.

Biscuits, cookies and confectionery

Crunchy nut biscuits

Overall timing 1¼ hours

Freezing Suitable

Makes about 24

8 oz	**Shelled hazelnuts**	**225 g**
6 oz	**Caster sugar**	**175 g**
¼ teasp	**Ground cinnamon**	**1.25 ml**
4	**Egg whites**	**4**
	Pinch of cream of tartar	
¼ teasp	**Vanilla essence**	**1.25 ml**

Preheat oven to 300°F (150°C) Gas 2. Grease and flour baking trays.

Spread shelled nuts on grill pan and toast on all sides till golden brown. Roughly chop nuts and put in a bowl with the sugar and the cinnamon.

In another bowl, whisk egg whites with cream of tartar and vanilla essence till very stiff. Gently fold in nut mixture. Scrape the egg/nut mixture into a greased heavy-based frying pan and cook over a very low heat for about 15 minutes, turning mixture constantly with a wooden spoon, until it is pale brown.

Put spoonfuls of the mixture on prepared baking trays, about 1 inch (2.5cm) apart. Bake for about 30 minutes, then reduce temperature to 250°F (130°C) Gas ½ and bake for a further 10 minutes until the biscuits are crisp.

Crunchy cookies

Overall timing 25 minutes

Freezing Suitable

Makes 24

5 oz	All-Bran	150 g
2 oz	Desiccated coconut	50 g
3 oz	Sultanas	75 g
2 tbsp	Golden syrup	2×15 ml
7fl oz	Can of condensed milk	200 ml

Preheat the oven to 375°F (190°C) Gas 5.

In a bowl mix together bran, coconut and sultanas. Stir the syrup into the condensed milk, then stir the mixture into other ingredients to make a fairly stiff consistency.

Place large spoonfuls of the mixture at well-spaced intervals on greased baking trays. Bake in two batches if necessary, towards top of oven for 15 minutes. Lift biscuits on to wire rack to cool.

Coconut surprises

Overall timing 25-30 minutes

Freezing Not suitable

Makes 35

4	Egg whites	4
6 oz	Icing sugar	175 g
6 oz	Desiccated coconut	175 g
1 oz	Self-raising flour	25 g

Preheat the oven to 375°F (190°C) Gas 5. Grease baking trays.

Beat the egg whites in a large bowl until very stiff. Gradually add the sifted icing sugar then lightly fold in the desiccated coconut and sifted flour until well combined.

Place small spoonfuls of the mixture on to baking trays, leaving plenty of room between each for spreading.

Cook for 15-20 minutes till lightly golden and cooked through. Cool on a wire rack.

Lemon crisps

Overall timing 20 minutes plus chilling

Freezing Suitable: before cooking

Makes 50

11 oz	Softened butter	300 g
3½ oz	Icing sugar	100 g
1 teasp	Salt	5 ml
2 teasp	Grated lemon rind	2×5 ml
14 oz	Plain flour	400 g

Preheat the oven to 400°F (200°C) Gas 6. Grease baking trays.

Cream together the butter, icing sugar, salt and lemon rind in a bowl. Mix in ¾ of the sifted flour, then turn mixture on to a board and work in the rest of the flour to make a smooth dough.

Shape into a roll about 10 inches (25 cm) long and 2 inches (5 cm) in diameter. Wrap in foil and chill for 2 hours.

Cut dough into 50 slices. Place on trays and bake for 10 minutes. Cool on wire racks, then decorate with lemon-flavoured glacé icing and sugared lemon slices.

Galettes bretonnes

Overall timing 20 minutes plus chilling

Freezing Suitable: before cooking

Makes 25

5 oz	Plain flour	150 g
	Pinch of salt	
2 oz	Icing sugar	50 g
3 oz	Melted butter	75 g
1	Egg	1
1 teasp	Vanilla essence	5 ml

Preheat the oven to 400°F (200°C) Gas 6. Grease baking trays.

Sift flour, salt and icing sugar into a bowl. Make a well in centre and pour in melted butter. Separate the egg. Add the yolk and essence to bowl and quickly mix to form a dough.

Knead into a ball, wrap and chill for 10 minutes.

Roll out dough to ¼ inch (6mm) thickness. Cut into 2 inch (5cm) circles and place on trays. Ridge tops with a fork, brush with beaten egg white (not necessary if icing).

Bake for 10 minutes till golden and cooked through. Cool on wire tray then ice and decorate if liked.

Peanut crunchies

Overall timing 20 minutes

Freezing Not suitable

Makes 30

3 oz	Margarine	75 g
6 oz	Caster sugar	175 g
1	Egg	1
6 oz	Raw peanuts	175 g
3 oz	Desiccated coconut	75 g
8 oz	Self-raising flour	225 g
1 tbsp	Cocoa	15 ml

Preheat the oven to 375°F (190°C) Gas 5. Grease baking trays.

Cream together the margarine and sugar till light and fluffy then add egg and beat well. Stir in the peanuts, coconut, sifted flour and cocoa to form a stiff mixture.

Roll into 30 balls and place on trays, leaving space between each for spreading. Cook towards the top of oven for 15 minutes. Cool on a wire rack.

Fruit and nutties

Overall timing 25 minutes

Freezing Not suitable

Makes 36

4 oz	Margarine	125 g
6 oz	Brown sugar	175 g
1	Egg	1
6 oz	Self-raising flour	175 g
½ teasp	Vanilla essence	2.5 ml
3 oz	Chopped nuts	75 g
6 oz	Glacé cherries	175 g

Preheat the oven to 375°F (190°C) Gas 5. Grease baking trays.

Cream together the margarine and brown sugar till soft and fluffy, add the egg and beat well. Stir in the sifted flour, vanilla essence, chopped nuts and 3 oz (75 g) of the glacé cherries, chopped.

Form the mixture into 2 rolls, 6 inches (15cm) long. Cut each into 18 slices, place on trays and decorate each with a halved glacé cherry. Bake for 15 minutes. Cool on a wire rack.

Petits sablés

Overall timing 20–22 minutes

Freezing Suitable: before cooking

Makes 25

5 oz	Plain flour	150 g
¼ teasp	Salt	1.25 ml
3 oz	Icing sugar	75 g
3 oz	Softened butter	75 g
2–3	Egg yolks	2–3

Preheat the oven to 375°F (190°C) Gas 5. Grease baking trays.

Sift flour, salt and icing sugar into a bowl. Work in the butter with a fork to form a breadcrumb-like texture.

If not piping mixture, mix in 2 egg yolks then form dough into a ball. Wrap and chill for 1 hour (freeze at this stage, if liked).

Roll out dough to ¼ inch (6mm) thickness. Cut out rounds, prick tops and place on trays.

If piping mixture, mix in 3 yolks. Place mixture in piping bag fitted with a large meringue nozzle and form high rosettes on trays (open freeze now, if liked).

Cook either biscuits for 10–12 minutes (more if frozen). Cool on wire racks.

Fruity barley delights

Overall timing 40 minutes

Freezing Not suitable

Makes about 24

4 oz	Pearl barley	125 g
1	Orange	1
8 oz	Dried apricots	225 g
1 tbsp	Orange flower water	15 ml
4 oz	Cottage cheese	125 g
4 tbsp	Ground almonds	4×15 ml
Coating		
2 oz	Sesame seeds	50 g
2 tbsp	Caster sugar	2×15 ml
1 teasp	Allspice	5 ml

Cover pearl barley with water. Bring to the boil and cook for 30 minutes or till barely tender.

Meanwhile, peel orange and cut into quarters. Remove pips and put flesh through the mincer along with the dried apricots. Add orange flower water, cottage cheese (squeezed dry in muslin) and ground almonds. Mix well.

When barley is cooked, drain well then return to pan and allow to steam dry for several minutes, stirring gently. Leave to cool, then add to other ingredients. Knead well with fingers to give an even consistency.

Form into about 24 small balls about 1 inch (2.5cm) diameter. Mix together sesame seeds, sugar and allspice on a plate. Roll balls in mixture till coated all over. Place in fridge till well chilled.

Chocolate hearts

Overall timing 1½ hours

Freezing Not suitable

Makes 40

4 oz	Bitter chocolate	125 g
3	Egg whites	3
12 oz	Caster sugar	350 g
12 oz	Ground almonds	350 g
½ teasp	Powdered ginger	2.5 ml
10 oz	Plain chocolate cake covering	275 g
½ oz	Coconut oil	15 g
5	Pieces of preserved ginger	5

Preheat the oven to 300°F (150°C) Gas 2. Grease baking trays.

Finely grate bitter chocolate. Beat egg whites in a bowl till stiff. Stir in sugar, ground almonds, grated chocolate and powdered ginger.

Mix well then knead with your hands. Sprinkle the work surface with sugar and roll out the dough to about ¼ inch (6mm) thickness. Cut out heart shapes. Knead trimmings, roll and cut out.

Place the hearts on trays and bake in the centre of the oven for 30 minutes. Remove from oven. Lift off trays and place on wire rack to cool.

Break the chocolate cake covering into a bowl and melt over a saucepan of gently boiling water. Stir in the coconut oil. Remove from heat and allow to cool slightly but not set.

Put foil beneath wire rack (this way you can scrape up leftovers and add to bowl). Spoon a little chocolate on to flat side of each heart. Allow to cool (refrigerate if necessary), then turn hearts over and coat rounded side. If some are uneven, reheat chocolate and apply a second coat. Sprinkle hearts with chopped ginger.

Chocolate fudge patties

Overall timing 2 hours

Freezing Suitable

Makes 12

8fl oz	Single cream	220 ml
1 lb	Caster sugar	450 g
3½ oz	Bitter chocolate	100 g
2 oz	Butter	50 g
1 teasp	Vanilla essence	5 ml

Put cream, sugar and broken-up chocolate into pan and heat till melted. Bring mixture to rapid boil and cook, stirring frequently, for 8 minutes until 238°F (115°C) is reached (soft ball stage). Remove pan from heat immediately. Plunge base into cold water. Chop butter and add. When mixture is fairly cool, beat continuously with a wooden spoon till mixture loses gloss and becomes firm. Beat in vanilla.

Pour into oiled patty tins and press firmly with back of wooden spoon. Allow to cool for about 1½ hours, then remove and chill till required.

Marzipan sweets

Overall timing 45 minutes

Freezing Suitable

Makes about 20

8 oz	Granulated sugar	225 g
3 tbsp	Water	3×15 ml
	Cream of tartar	
6 oz	Ground almonds	175 g
	Grated rind of 1 lemon	
2	Egg whites	2
3 oz	Icing sugar	75 g
1	Egg yolk	1
2 oz	Candied lemon peel	50 g

Heat sugar with water till dissolved. Bring to boil and add pinch of cream of tartar. Heat to 240°F (116°C), then remove from heat and stir until syrup looks, "grainy". Add the almonds and lemon rind.

Lightly beat egg whites, add to syrup and stir over a low heat for 1–2 minutes. Turn out on to an oiled baking tray. Sift icing sugar and work in with a palate knife. Cool.

Preheat oven to 375°F (190°C) Gas 5. Knead mixture till smooth, adding more icing sugar if necessary to make a firm paste. Form into small balls and flatten slightly. Brush tops with egg yolk and sprinkle half with half diced peel. Top with plain rounds and press centres to make a small indentation.

Bake for 10–15 minutes until pale golden. Press remaining peel on top of sweets. Leave to cool before serving.

Coffee petits fours

Overall timing 30 minutes plus overnight chilling

Freezing Suitable: without sugar coating and walnuts

Makes 24

24	Boudoir biscuits	24
2 oz	Icing sugar	50 g
2	Egg yolks	2
8fl oz	Strong black coffee	220 ml
2 oz	Softened butter	50 g
2 tbsp	Coffee crystals	2×15 ml
24	Walnuts	24

Crush biscuits finely in a bowl with the end of a rolling-pin (or place in a plastic bag and crush). In another bowl, whisk together the icing sugar, sifted, and egg yolks till pale and fluffy. Add coffee, then gradually mix in the biscuit crumbs and butter. When well combined, place in fridge and leave overnight.

The next day, make little balls with the mixture. Roll to coat in sugar crystals and top each one with a walnut. Place in paper cases and chill till ready to serve after dinner.

Index